Homemade
pies

Homemade
pies

CATHERINE ATKINSON

 **Bounty**
Books

First published in Great Britain in 2005 by
MQ Publications, a division of Octopus Publishing Group Ltd

This edition published in 2011 by Bounty Books,
a division of Octopus Publishing Group Ltd
Endeavour House
189 Shaftesbury Avenue
London WC2H 8JY
www.octopusbooks.co.uk

An Hachette UK Company
www.hachette.co.uk

Reprinted 2011

Both US and metric measurements are given for the recipes.
Use one set of measurements only, not a mixture of both.

ISBN: 978-0-753721-45-2

A CIP catalogue record for this book is available from the
British Library

Printed and bound in China

Contents

Introduction

Few can resist the tantalizing taste and aroma of a steaming fruit-laden pie with melt-in-the-mouth buttery pastry, or a slice of velvety-smooth custard, sharp lemon, or creamy chocolate tart. Eating a good pie is an enjoyable experience, but making your own is infinitely more satisfying.

Pie making is an important part of our heritage, "As American as Apple Pie," and conjures up fond memories of the pies our mom and grandma used to bake. In an age where we are more likely to buy ready-made meals and fast food, nothing comforts more than a homemade pie. Although some may find the thought of pastry making daunting, you don't have to be an experienced cook to succeed; you'll find all the necessary information here, from making different types of pastry to rolling out and lining tart pans and creating single- and double-crust pies,

so that even the first-time cook can achieve excellent results. Of course, not all pies have a pastry crust; cookie crumb and Graham cracker crusts are incredibly quick and easy to prepare, and work beautifully with creamy fillings; indeed the secret of all good pies is the clever combination of the right crust and filling.

The potential combinations are limited only by your imagination. From all-time American classics to more contemporary choices, here you'll find an inspirational collection of sweet pies for every possible occasion.

Tips for Succesful Pie Making

Equipment

Using the correct baking equipment simplifies and enhances pie making, but few specialist implements are essential. You probably already possess the basic items: standard measuring cups and spoons or accurate weighing scales, a calibrated pitcher, a good-sized mixing bowl, a fine strainer, and a few sharp knifes. Other important items include:

Rolling pin: A thick, heavy one is best for rolling out pastry, although marble rolling pins are cooler.

Timer: Vital when pie making.

Pie plates and dishes: in glass or porcelain, which have an unglazed base to allow heat to penetrate. These are especially useful for single-crust pies.

Tart pans: The best are metal with fluted sides, which are easier to line. Loose bases will simplify removal.

Pastry brush: for even glazing.

Baking beans: for "baking blind." Choose ceramic or aluminum ones, which last forever and are good heat conductors, or simply use dried beans or pulses.

Wire rack: to allow air to circulate and prevent sogginess when cooling pie shells.

Ingredients

Most pastry doughs are created from three simple ingredients: flour, shortening, and water. Used in the correct proportions and handled correctly, these make delicious, flaky pie crusts. The addition of egg or egg yolk, sweetener, and flavoring are ways of altering the taste and texture of the final product.

Traditional pastry calls for all-purpose flour, and no other type should be used unless specified in the recipe. Self-rising flour produces a softer pastry and may be used in a suet-crust. Whole wheat makes a much heavier dough, but is sometimes used together with all-purpose flour. Pastry can be made with one fat or a mixture. Butter on its own gives an excellent flavor and color. If margarine is preferred it should be the hard-block variety. White vegetable fat, or shortening, makes shorter, more flaky pastry and is often used with butter in equal amounts.

Making Perfect Pastry

There are many different types of pastry, from buttery, layered puff, and flaky pastry to paper-thin phyllo, also known as strudel pastry. Shortcrust is probably the best known and most frequently used for pie making. While it's the simplest of all pastries, it needs a cool, light hand and you should avoid overhandling the dough or it will become tough.

When making shortcrust pastry, use twice as much flour as fat in weight. To line a 10in/25cm tart pan you'll need 1½ cups/225g flour and 1 stick/115g fat.

1. If making by hand, sift the flour and salt together into a mixing bowl, then cut the fat into the flour using a pastry blender, or use your fingertips to rub it in. Shake the bowl every now and then to bring any large pieces of fat to the top. Blend until the mixture resembles fine bread crumbs.

2. Sprinkle cold water evenly over the dry ingredients (you'll need 3 to 4 tbsp for the above quantities). Add the smaller amount of water first, and mix lightly with a fork or round-bladed knife until the dough comes together. Add the extra water if the mixture is still too dry.

3. Gather the dough into a ball and knead on a lightly floured surface for just a few seconds until smooth. Wrap the dough in plastic wrap and chill for 30 minutes, until firm, but not too stiff to roll.

Once you've mastered shortcrust, you can flavor the dough in endless ways; a little grated citrus peel, a few drops of vanilla or almond extract, or a sprinkling of ground spices are just a few ideas.

Six steps to shortcrust success:

1. Always sift flour to remove lumps and incorporate air.

2. When making pastry, use fat that is cool but not hard.

3. Always chill shortcrust before rolling, after rolling, and before baking. This allows the gluten to "relax," preventing shrinkage.

4. After chilling pastry, leave at room temperature for a few minutes before rolling out.

5. Roll pastry in short, gentle strokes, lightly and evenly in one direction only. Keep turning it to stop it sticking.

6. If you need a large amount of pastry (if making several pies), make it in batches.

Lining a Tart Pan

1. On a lightly floured surface, roll out the pastry to a thickness of ⅛in/3mm and to a circle about 2 to 3in/5 to 7.5cm larger than the tart pan, depending on the depth of the pan.

2. Lift the pastry with the rolling pin and ease it into the pan. Press the pastry against the side of the pan so that there are no gaps. Roll the rolling pin over the top of the pan to cut off the excess dough.

3. Prick the base of the dough liberally, and then chill for at least 10 minutes, to prevent puffing and shrinkage during baking.

Baking Blind

This is used either to partly cook an empty pie shell, so that it does not become soggy when the filling is added, or to completely bake a pie shell when the filling isn't baked.

1. To bake the pie shell partially, line with baking parchment or foil and fill with dried or baking beans. Bake at 400°F/200°C for 10 to 15 minutes.

Remove the paper or foil and beans. Brush with beaten egg, if the filling is moist, to seal the base. Bake for 5 minutes more.

2. To fully bake the pie shell, follow the above, but bake for 10 minutes after the paper or foil are removed, or until golden brown. Cool before filling.

Baking Tips

1. Always bake pie shells and double-crust pies on a heated baking sheet. This helps to crispen the pastry base and also catch any drips should the filled shell or pie bubble over.

2. If you find any small holes in a cooked pie shell, repair them by brushing with beaten egg, then return to the oven for 2 to 3 minutes to seal.

3. If the pastry has fully browned before the filling is cooked, protect it with foil. Cover single and double-crust pies completely, making a hole in the foil to let steam escape. On open pie shells, cover the pastry edge only with strips of foil.

Keeping and Freezing Pastry

Uncooked puff, shortcrust, and most other pastries can be stored chilled for several days in plastic wrap to prevent them from drying out. Pastry may also be frozen for several weeks; thaw in the refrigerator overnight, then leave at room temperature for 15 minutes before rolling out. You can also freeze sheets of rolled out pastry, placed on baking parchment on a baking sheet and covered with plastic wrap. Unbaked pie shells will keep covered in the refrigerator for 2 to 3 days, or for a week in the freezer. Fully baked pie shells may be frozen or kept in an airtight container for a day or two.

CHAPTER ONE

Old-Fashioned Fruit Pies

Grandma's Apple Pie

With its domed top, tender pastry, and delicious spicy filling, this is a real winner. Enjoy it hot or cold, with whipped cream or ice cream.

Serves 8

3 cups/450g all-purpose flour
½ tsp salt
1 stick/115g butter
6 tbsp/100g vegetable shortening
Milk, to glaze
Sugar, to dust

For the filling:
2lb/900g cooking apples, peeled, cored, and thinly sliced
2 tsp lemon juice
6 tbsp raisins
1 tsp pared orange peel
1 cup/225g light brown sugar
4 tsp cornstarch
1 tsp ground cinnamon
1 tsp freshly grated nutmeg
4 tsp butter

1. Put a baking sheet in the oven and preheat to 400°F/200°C. Make the pastry by sifting the flour and salt in a bowl, rubbing in the butter and shortening, then adding just enough iced water to bind. Wrap in plastic wrap and chill for 30 minutes.

2. To make the filling, put the sliced apples into a bowl. Toss with the lemon juice, then add all the remaining filling ingredients, except the butter, and mix lightly.

3. Roll out just less than half the pastry on a lightly floured surface and use to line a 10in/25cm pie plate. Add the filling, mounding it into the center, then dot with the butter.

4. Roll out the remaining pastry and make a lid for the pie. Seal and crimp the edges and cut two steam vents. Brush the surface lightly with milk and sprinkle with sugar. Bake for 15 minutes then reduce the oven temperature to 350°F/180°C and bake for 20 minutes more. Serve hot or cold.

Freeform Spiced Plum Pie

Try to buy plump, ripe plums for this recipe—it will give the best flavor to the pie. Serve with whipped cream.

Serves 6–8

½ cup/75g pecan nuts, very
   finely chopped
1⅓ cups/200g all-purpose flour
1⅓ sticks/150g sweet butter, diced
½ cup/120ml sour cream
Whipped cream, to serve

For the filling:
2lb/900g ripe plums, pitted and quartered
½ cup/115g light brown sugar
1 tsp ground cinnamon
½ tsp ground ginger
Pinch freshly grated nutmeg

1. To make the pastry, place the pecans, flour, and butter in a food processor and process briefly until the mixture forms very coarse bread crumbs. Add the sour cream and process for another 4 to 5 seconds. Alternatively, rub the butter into the flour using your hands or a pastry cutter and mix in the cream.

2. Turn the pastry out onto a lightly floured board and bring the mixture together with your hands. Wrap in plastic wrap and chill for 20 minutes.

3. To make the filling, place the plums in a bowl and mix with the brown sugar and spices.

4. Roll out the pastry on a lightly floured surface into a circle 14in/35cm in diameter, and place on a nonstick baking sheet. Pile the plums into the center of the pastry, leaving a 3in/7.5cm margin.

5. Bring up the sides of the pastry to half-cover the plums. Preheat the oven to 400°F/200°C. Let the pie chill for 20 minutes, and then bake for 40 to 45 minutes. Serve with whipped cream.

Gooseberry Pie

This deliciously crumbly cornmeal pastry complements the tart gooseberries perfectly.

Serves 6

1⅓ cups/200g all-purpose flour
Pinch salt
½ cup/60g stoneground cornmeal
¼ cup/50g light brown sugar
Scant 1⅓ sticks/140g butter, diced
3–4 tbsp cold water
1 egg, beaten
Whipped cream or custard, to serve

For the filling:
1lb 9oz/700g gooseberries
4 tbsp sugar, plus extra to dust

1. Sift the flour into a bowl with the salt, and add the cornmeal and sugar. Rub or cut in the butter until the mixture resembles fine bread crumbs. Add 3 tbsp cold water and mix to a firm dough, adding a little more water, if necessary.

2. Turn the dough onto a lightly floured surface and knead briefly, until the dough is smooth. Form into a neat ball, wrap in plastic wrap, and chill for 20 minutes.

3. To make the filling, mix the gooseberries with 4 tbsp of sugar. Divide the pastry into two pieces, one slightly larger than the other. Roll out the larger piece and use to line an 8in/20cm shallow pie plate. Spoon the gooseberries into the pan. Brush the rim of the pastry with a little beaten egg.

4. Roll out the remaining piece of pastry and lay it over the gooseberries. Press down and seal the edges. Cut off any overhanging pastry, crimp the edges, and make a steam hole in the top of the pie. Chill for 20 minutes. Meanwhile, preheat the oven to 375°F/190°C.

5. Brush the top of the pie with a little more egg and dust with sugar. Bake for 40 minutes, or until golden. Serve warm with whipped cream or custard.

Cherry Pie

An all-time classic. If you are short of time, try canned pitted cherries.

Serves 6–8

2½ cups/375g all-purpose flour
½ tsp salt
1¼ sticks/125g sweet butter, diced
¾ cup/120g vegetable shortening
2–3 tbsp cold water
Milk, for brushing

For the filling:
1¾ lb/800g pitted fresh or canned
    cherries
¼ cup/50g sugar, plus extra for
    sprinkling
2 tbsp cornstarch
½ tsp ground cinnamon
Pinch freshly grated nutmeg

1. Sift the flour and salt into a bowl. Rub in the fat until the mixture resembles fine bread crumbs. Add 2 tbsp water and mix to a firm dough, adding more water, if necessary. Knead briefly until smooth. Form into a ball, wrap in plastic wrap, and chill for 20 minutes. Meanwhile, preheat the oven to 400°F/200°C.

2. To make the filling, mix the cherries with the sugar, cornstarch, and spices.

3. Divide the pastry into 2 pieces, one a little larger than the other. Roll out the larger piece of pastry and line an 8 x 1½ in/20 x 4cm diameter deep pan. Spoon the filling into the pie. Brush the edges of the pastry with a little milk.

4. Roll out the remaining pastry and use to make a lid, pressing the edges together to seal. Trim the excess pastry and crimp or score the edges. Score the surface of the pie to decorate. Chill for 20 minutes then brush the top with extra milk and sprinkle with sugar.

5. Bake for 45 minutes, or until golden. Let stand for 5 minutes before serving.

Four Berry Pie

Make the most of luscious summer fruits by combining them in this fragrant pie. Raspberries, strawberries, blueberries, and blackberries are the traditional combination, but you can use fewer varieties or substitute some red or black currants if you prefer.

Serves 6

2 cups/300g all-purpose flour
1 tbsp sugar
1 tsp grated orange peel
1½ sticks/175g butter, diced
2½–3 tbsp cold water
Sweetened whipped cream, to serve

For the filling:
1 cup/250g raspberries
1 cup/175g blackberries
¾ cup/115g hulled strawberries,
   quartered
¾ cup/115g blueberries
¼ cup/50g sugar, or to taste

1 tbsp cornstarch
Beaten egg, to glaze
1 tbsp confectioners' sugar

1. Sift the flour and sugar into a mixing bowl, and then stir in the orange peel. Rub or cut in the butter until the mixture resembles fine bread crumbs. Sprinkle over 2½ tbsp of the water and mix to a firm dough, adding the remaining water if needed. Wrap in plastic wrap and chill for 30 minutes.

2. To make the filling, put the fruit into a bowl with the quartered strawberries at the top, then sprinkle over the sugar. (Use a little more sugar if some of the fruit is slightly tart.) After a few minutes, gently toss the fruit with your hands to coat it in the sugar. Leave for 20 minutes, or until a small pool of fruit juice has collected at the bottom of the bowl. Meanwhile, put a baking sheet in the oven and preheat to 400°F/200°C.

3. Roll out about two thirds of the pastry on a lightly floured surface to a circle about 1½ in/4cm larger all round than a shallow 8-9in/20-23cm pie dish. Line the pie dish, leaving an overhang of pastry, and then dampen the edge with a little water.

4. Carefully transfer the fruit to the pie shell using your hands. Blend the cornstarch and the fruit juice at the bottom of the bowl together to form a smooth paste, and drizzle this over the fruit.

5. Roll out the remaining pastry to make a lid and use to cover the pie, pressing the edges together well to seal. Trim the excess pastry with a knife. Crimp the edge of the pie and make decorations from the re-rolled pastry trimmings.

6. Brush the pie with beaten egg to glaze, then sprinkle over the confectioners' sugar. Slash the top twice or make small holes with a skewer to let steam escape. Bake for 35 to 45 minutes, or until the pastry is a deep golden brown. Let the pie settle for 10 minutes before slicing and serving with sweetened whipped cream.

Rhubarb Pie

Serves 6–8

1½ cups/225g all-purpose flour
½ cup/55g confectioners' sugar
Finely grated peel of 1 orange
1⅓ sticks/150g butter, diced
1 small egg, lightly beaten

For the filling:
6 cups/675g rhubarb, chopped
2 tsp water
6 tbsp/75g sugar
3 tbsp cornstarch
Juice 2 medium oranges
2 egg yolks

1. Sift the flour and sugar into a bowl. Stir in the orange peel. Rub in the butter until the mixture resembles fine bread crumbs. Add all but 1 tbsp of the egg, then mix to a dough. Knead, then wrap and chill for 30 minutes.

2. Put a baking sheet in the oven and preheat to 400°F/200°C. Roll out the pastry on a lightly floured surface and use to line a 10in/25cm loose-bottomed tart pan. Chill for 15 minutes.

3. Line the pie shell with baking parchment and baking beans. Bake blind for 15 minutes. Remove the parchment and beans, and brush with the reserved beaten egg. Cook for 5 minutes more. Reduce the oven temperature to 325°F/160°C.

4. Put the rhubarb, water, and half the sugar in a pan. Cover and cook over low heat for 10 minutes, or until there is a lot of juice.

5. Blend the cornstarch with the orange juice and stir into the rhubarb off the heat. Slowly bring to a boil, stirring, until thickened. Let cool for 5 minutes.

6. Beat the egg yolks in a bowl with the remaining sugar. Stir in a spoonful of the rhubarb juice, then stir the egg mixture into the rhubarb. Spoon into the pie shell. Bake for 20 to 25 minutes, until the rhubarb is tender and the filling is softly set.

Two-crust Prune Pie

It's worth keeping dried prunes in the pantry so that this tasty pie can be made at a moment's notice.

Serves 6–8

1½ cups/225g all-purpose flour
Pinch salt
½ tsp ground cinnamon
1 stick/115g butter, or half butter/
  half white vegetable fat, diced
3–4 tbsp cold water
1 tbsp milk, to glaze
1 tbsp sugar
Custard or cream, to serve

For the filling:
2¼ cups/450g dried prunes
1 tbsp all-purpose flour
¼ cup/50g sugar
2 tsp lemon juice
2 tsp butter

1. To make the filling, put the prunes in a large bowl and pour over enough near-boiling water to just cover them. Let soak for 2 hours.

2. To make the pastry, sift the flour, salt, and cinnamon into a bowl and rub or cut in the fat until the mixture resembles fine bread crumbs. Sprinkle 3 tbsp water over the surface and mix to a firm dough, adding the remaining water if necessary. Knead briefly, then wrap in plastic wrap and chill for 30 minutes.

3. Drain the prunes, reserving 1 cup/240ml of the soaking liquid. Halve the prunes and remove the pits. Blend the flour, sugar, lemon juice, and a little of the soaking liquid to a paste in a pan. Stir in the remaining soaking liquid, then add the prunes and butter. Bring to a boil and simmer for 1 to 2 minutes, or until thickened, stirring constantly. Remove from the heat and let cool.

4. Put a baking sheet in the oven and preheat to 375°F/190°C. Roll out two thirds of the pastry to a circle about 1½in/4cm larger all around than a shallow 8-9in/20-23cm pie dish. Ease the dough into the pie dish, leaving an overhang of pastry.

5. Spoon the prune mixture into the pie shell, then dampen the pastry edge with water. Roll out the remaining pastry to make a lid and use to cover the pie, pressing the edges together well to seal. Trim the excess pastry with a knife.

6. Crimp the edge of the pie, then decorate by cutting pastry leaves from the re-rolled trimmings and attaching these with water or milk. Glaze the pie with milk, and sprinkle with sugar. Slash the top twice, or make small holes with a skewer. Bake for 35 to 40 minutes, or until the pastry is golden brown and crisp. Serve hot, with custard or cream.

Blackberry and Apple Pie

Black currants, cranberries, or red gooseberries can be used in this pie as a substitute and are equally delicious.

Serves 6–8

2½ cups/375g all-purpose flour
½ cup/55g confectioners' sugar
1¼ sticks/125g butter
1 egg, plus 1 egg yolk
Milk, to glaze
Sugar, for sprinkling

For the filling:
3 small tart apples, peeled, cored, and thinly sliced
1lb 9oz/700g blackberries
1 cup/200g sugar
1 tbsp cornstarch
½ tsp ground allspice
½ tsp freshly grated nutmeg

1. Sift the flour and confectioners' sugar into a bowl. Rub in the butter until the mixture resembles bread crumbs. Add the egg and egg yolk, and mix quickly to a rough dough. Wrap and let it rest in a cool place (not the refrigerator) for 20 minutes.

2. Put a baking sheet in the oven and preheat to 400°F/200°C. Put the apple slices in a bowl and add the blackberries, sugar, cornstarch, allspice, and nutmeg. Toss gently to mix.

3. Roll out just less than half the pastry on a lightly floured surface, and line a 10in/25cm pie plate. Spoon the filling on top.

4. Roll out the remaining dough to a circle 1in/2.5cm wider than the rim of the pan. Moisten the rim of the pie shell with water, then place the pastry on top. Seal and trim off the excess pastry. Crimp the edges and cut a steam vent in the top. Glaze the pie with milk, and sprinkle with sugar.

5. Bake for 15 minutes then reduce the temperature to 350°F/180°C and bake for 20 to 25 minutes more. Serve warm.

Grape Pie

This single-crust pie looks stunning made in a glass pie dish, so that the fruit and bubbling juices can be seen. Choose seedless grapes if possible.

Serves 6

Generous 1 cup/175g all-purpose flour
Pinch salt
¼ tsp ground ginger
7 tbsp/90g chilled butter, or half
**   butter/half white vegetable fat**
2 tbsp cold water
1 tbsp Demerara sugar, to sprinkle
Custard or cream, to serve

For the filling:
4½ cups/675g white or red grapes,
**   preferably seedless**
¼ cup/50g Demerara sugar, or to taste
2 tbsp cornstarch
3 tbsp grape, apple, or orange juice
1 tbsp butter
1 tbsp milk

1. Sift the flour, salt, and ginger into a bowl and rub or cut in the fat until the mixture resembles fine bread crumbs. Sprinkle over the water and mix to a firm dough. Knead briefly, then wrap in plastic wrap and chill for 30 minutes. Meanwhile, preheat the oven to 400°F/200°C.

2. For the filling, halve the grapes, if large, removing the pips if necessary, and put them in a bowl with the sugar. Blend the cornstarch with the juice and pour over the grapes, and then toss the mixture gently with your hands to ensure all the fruit is coated.

3. Using an inverted 4 cup/1 liter dish as a guide, roll out the pastry on a lightly floured surface until it is 2in/5cm larger all around than the dish. Cut off a 1in/2.5cm strip from around the edge. Moisten the rim of the pie dish and position the strip on the rim. Brush with water.

4. Stir the grape mixture, and then tip into the pie dish, piling up the grapes in the center so that the filling is slightly rounded. Dot the top of the fruit with butter. Place the pastry lid on top, pressing the edges together to seal. Trim off the excess pastry and make a steam hole in the top of the pie.

5. Knock up the pastry edge by holding the blunt edge of a knife horizontally against the rim and tapping sharply, then flute or crimp the edge or press a pattern with the back of a floured fork. Brush with milk, to glaze, then sprinkle with Demerara sugar.

6. Bake the pie for 15 minutes, then reduce the temperature to 350°F/180°C and bake for another 20 to 30 minutes, or until the pastry is dark golden and crisp. Serve hot or warm with custard or cream.

Peach Cobbler

Serves 4–6

2¼ lb/1kg firm ripe peaches or
    nectarines (or canned equivalent)
3 tbsp cornstarch
Generous ½ cup/115g sugar
¼ tsp ground cinnamon
Juice 1 lemon
¼ stick/25g butter, diced

For the topping:
1½ cups/225g self-rising flour
Pinch salt
1 tsp baking powder
3 tbsp/40g butter, diced
Scant ⅔ cup/150ml milk
Beaten egg, to glaze
1 tbsp confectioners' sugar
Custard or cream, to serve

1. Preheat the oven to 325°F/160°C. For
the filling, drop a few peaches at a time
into a pan of boiling water, leave for 30 to 40
seconds, then transfer to a bowl of cold water.
Peel and slice the fruit, removing the pits.

2. Put the fruit slices in a bowl. Blend the
cornstarch with the sugar and cinnamon,
and sprinkle over. Gently toss together then
transfer to a 9in/23cm pie dish. Dot the top
with butter. Cover with foil, then bake for
20 minutes.

3. For the pastry, sift the flour, salt, and baking
powder together into a bowl. Rub in the butter
until the mixture resembles bread crumbs.
Stir in enough milk to give a fairly soft dough.

4. Remove the peaches from the oven and
stir. Increase the temperature to 425°F/220°C.
Roll out the dough on a lightly floured surface
until slightly larger than the pie dish. Lightly
brush the edges of the pie dish with water,
and then place the lid over the peach filling.

5. Brush the top of the cobbler with beaten
egg and make two small slits in the top.
Bake for 12 to 15 minutes, or until the top
is well-risen and golden brown. Dust
with confectioners' sugar and serve hot
with custard or cream.

Cherry Cinnamon Cobbler

This warming pudding is topped with a thick crust; perfect fuel for a cold winter's day.

Serves 4–6

2¼ lb/1kg pitted black cherries in
    heavy syrup
2oz/55g dried cherries
½ cup/100g light brown sugar
2 tbsp cornstarch
2 tbsp cold water

For the topping:
1⅓ cups/200g all-purpose flour
Pinch salt
2 tsp baking powder
1 tsp ground cinnamon
½ cup/100g brown sugar
¾ stick/85g butter, melted
½ cup/120ml milk

1. Put a baking sheet in the oven and preheat to 375°F/190°C. Drain the cherries, reserving the syrup. Place them with the dried cherries in a large pie dish. Place 2½ cups/600ml of the syrup in a pan and add the brown sugar. Slowly bring to a boil, stirring until the sugar has dissolved.

2. Mix the cornstarch with the water and stir into the syrup. Cook for 1 to 2 minutes, or until the syrup thickens. Pour the syrup over the cherries.

3. To make the topping, combine the flour, salt, baking powder, cinnamon, and sugar in a bowl. Stir in the melted butter and milk and mix well. Spoon dollops of the batter over the cherries.

4. Bake for 35 to 40 minutes, or until the topping is risen and golden.

· · · · · · · · · · ·

CHAPTER TWO

Sweet and Sticky Pies

Shoofly Pie

*When making this rich, sticky treat
from the Deep South it's important to
work quickly while mixing the
molasses and soda, and to bake the
pie straight away.*

Serves 6–8

Generous 1 cup/175g all-purpose flour
Pinch salt
7 tbsp/90g butter, diced
About 2 tbsp cold water
Custard or cream, to serve

For the filling:
2 eggs, lightly beaten
¾ cup/115g all-purpose flour
½ cup/115g packed dark brown sugar
¼ tsp each ground ginger and nutmeg
½ tsp ground cinnamon
⅔ stick/75g butter, diced
½ cup/185g molasses
Scant ½ cup/110ml boiling water
½ tsp baking soda

1. Sift the flour and salt into a mixing bowl.
Rub or cut in the butter until the mixture
resembles fine bread crumbs. Sprinkle the
water over the flour mixture, and stir
together to make a firm dough. Knead
briefly, then wrap in plastic wrap, and
chill for 30 minutes. Meanwhile, put a
baking sheet in the oven and preheat
to 400°F/200°C.

2. Roll out the pastry on a lightly
floured surface and use to line a 9in/23cm
pie plate. Trim and flute the edges, then
prick the base all over with a fork. Chill
for 15 minutes.

3. Line the pie shell with baking parchment
and fill with baking beans. Bake blind for
15 minutes. Remove the parchment and
beans, brush the base with 1 tsp beaten
egg from the filling, and bake for another
5 minutes. Remove from the oven and
reduce the temperature to 375°F/190°C.

4. To make the filling, sift the flour into a mixing bowl. Stir in the brown sugar and spices. Rub or cut in the butter until the mixture resembles coarse bread crumbs. Sprinkle about a third over the base of the pie shell.

5. Beat the eggs with the molasses in a bowl. Pour the boiling water into a large pitcher and stir in the baking soda (it will froth up, so make sure there's room for this). Immediately pour into the egg mixture and beat the mixture together.

6. Quickly pour the mixture into the pie shell and sprinkle evenly with the remaining spice mixture. Return the pie to the oven and bake for 30 to 35 minutes, or until firm and browned. Serve warm or at room temperature with custard or cream.

Chocolate Chip and Peanut Butter Pie

Serves 8

Generous 1 cup/175g all-purpose flour
Pinch salt
7 tbsp/90g chilled butter, diced
2 tbsp cold water

For the filling:
3 eggs, lightly beaten
½ cup/115g smooth peanut butter
½ cup/115g packed brown sugar
⅔ cup/200g light corn syrup
1 tsp vanilla extract
⅔ cup/100g semisweet chocolate chips

1. Sift the flour and salt into a bowl. Rub in the butter until the mixture resembles fine bread crumbs. Sprinkle over the water and mix to a firm dough. Knead until smooth, wrap, and chill for 30 minutes. Meanwhile, put a baking sheet in the oven and preheat to 400°F/200°C.

2. Roll out the pastry on a lightly floured surface and use to line a shallow 9in/23cm pie plate. Prick the base all over with a fork, then crimp the edge or decorate with the fork. Chill for 10 minutes.

3. Line the pie shell with baking parchment and baking beans. Bake for 15 minutes. Remove the parchment and beans, brush the base with 1 tsp beaten egg from the filling, and bake for 5 minutes more. Reduce the temperature to 350°F/180°C.

4. For the filling, combine the peanut butter, sugar, syrup, eggs, and vanilla extract in a bowl. Stir in the chocolate chips. Pour the filling into the pie shell and bake for 30 minutes. The center will still be slightly wobbly, but will firm up as it cools.

5. Remove from the oven and let stand for 15 minutes on a wire rack, then remove the pie from the pan and cool before serving.

Coffee and Walnut Pie

If you like pecan pie, you'll love this coffee-maple-walnut alternative.

Serves 4–6

1 cup/150g all-purpose flour
Pinch salt
⅔ stick/75g butter, diced
2–3 tbsp cold water

For the filling:
¾ cup/180ml maple syrup
1 tbsp instant coffee granules
1 tbsp boiling water
¼ stick/25g butter, softened
⅔ cup/130g golden brown sugar
3 eggs, beaten
1 tsp vanilla extract
⅔ cup/75g walnut halves
Whipped cream or ice cream, to serve

1. Sift the flour and salt into a bowl. Rub or cut in the butter until the mixture resembles fine bread crumbs. Add 2 tbsp cold water and, using a narrow spatula, start to bring the dough together, adding a little more water, if necessary. Turn the dough onto a lightly floured surface and knead briefly, until the dough is smooth. Form into a neat ball, wrap in plastic wrap, and chill for 20 minutes.

2. Roll the pastry into a rough circle at least 2in/5cm in diameter larger than a loose-bottomed 9in/23cm fluted tart pan. Gently roll the pastry onto the rolling pin, then unroll it over the pan to cover. Carefully press the pastry into the edge of the pan, removing any overhanging pastry with a knife. Prick the base all over with a fork. Chill for 20 minutes. Meanwhile, put a baking sheet in the oven and preheat to 400°F/200°C.

3. Line the pie shell with baking parchment and fill with baking beans.

Transfer to the oven and bake for
12 minutes. Remove the baking beans
and parchment and cook for another
10 minutes, or until golden. Remove from
the oven and let cool. Reduce the oven
temperature to 350°F/180°C.

4. To make the filling, put the maple syrup
into a pan and heat until almost boiling.
Mix the coffee granules with the boiling
water, stirring until they have completely
dissolved. Stir this mixture into the maple
syrup. Leave until just warm.

5. Mix the butter with the sugar until
combined, and then gradually beat in the
eggs. Add the cooled maple syrup mixture
with the vanilla extract, and stir well.

6. Arrange the walnut halves in the base
of the pie shell, then carefully pour in the
filling. Transfer to the oven and bake for
30 to 35 minutes, or until browned and
firm. Let cool for about 10 minutes. Serve
with whipped cream or ice cream.

Transparent Pie

This tempting pie separates into two layers as it cooks. Cut into the pale foamy surface to reveal a translucent lemon jelly-like layer beneath. The cream cheese pastry contrasts well with the sweetness of the filling.

Serves 8–10

1 cup/150g all-purpose flour
Pinch salt
1 tsp sugar
½ cup/115g whole cream cheese,
    at room temperature
1 stick/115g butter, at room
    temperature, diced

For the filling:
1 tbsp warm water
¾ cup/175g packed light brown sugar
½ stick/50g butter, softened
3 eggs, lightly beaten
⅓ cup/100g light corn syrup
2 tbsp lemon juice
¼ tsp freshly grated nutmeg (optional)

1. Sift the flour, salt, and sugar into a bowl. Add the cream cheese and butter. Using the back of a fork, mix the butter and cream cheese into the flour to make a soft dough. Lightly knead into a ball, and then flatten slightly to make rolling out easier. Wrap in plastic wrap and chill for 1 hour.

2. Put a baking sheet in the oven and preheat to 400°F/200°C. Roll out the pastry on a lightly floured surface and use to line a shallow 9½in/24cm tart pan. Prick the base all over with a fork, then chill for 10 minutes.

3. Line the pie shell with baking parchment and baking beans. Bake blind for 15 minutes. Remove the parchment and beans, and then bake for another 5 minutes. Reduce the temperature to 325°F/160°C.

4. To make the filling, stir the water and brown sugar together in a bowl. Add the butter and beat the mixture until light.

Gradually beat in the eggs, and then stir in
the syrup and lemon juice.

5. Pour the filling into the pie shell and
sprinkle with grated nutmeg, if using. Bake
for 30 to 35 minutes, or until the tip of a
knife comes out clean when inserted into the
center of the pie. Cool on a wire rack for a
few minutes before removing the pie from
the pan. Serve warm or cold.

Cook's Tips:
- This pie is sometimes made with
  currant or another tart jelly, which
  gives it a sharper flavor.
- Substitute 3 tbsp jelly, melted over
  low heat, for an equal amount of
  the light corn syrup.

Carolina Vinegar Pie

Serves 8

Generous 1 cup/175g all-purpose flour
Pinch salt
½ stick/50g chilled butter, diced
3 tbsp/40g white vegetable shortening
2 tbsp cold water

For the filling:
2 eggs, lightly beaten
Generous 1 cup/225g sugar
2 tbsp all-purpose flour
1–2 tbsp cider or white wine vinegar,
   to taste
1 cup/240ml water
1 tbsp butter
Pared strip lemon peel

1. Sift the flour and salt into a bowl. Rub in the fat until the mixture resembles fine bread crumbs. Sprinkle over the water and mix to a firm dough. Knead until smooth, wrap, and chill for 30 minutes. Put a baking sheet in the oven and preheat to 400°F/200°C. Roll out the pastry on a floured surface and use to line a shallow 9in/23cm tart pan. Prick the base all over with a fork. Chill for 10 minutes.

2. Line the pie shell with baking parchment and fill with baking beans. Bake for 15 minutes. Remove the parchment and beans, brush the base with 1 tsp beaten egg from the filling, and bake for 8 minutes more. Reduce the temperature to 300°F/150°C.

3. Put the sugar and flour in a pan and blend with the vinegar and a little of the water. Gradually beat in the remaining water, then the eggs. Add the butter and lemon peel.

4. Cook over very low heat, stirring constantly until the mixture thickens. Remove the lemon peel, pour the filling into the pie shell, and bake for 15 to 20 minutes, or until lightly set.

5. Remove from the oven and place on a wire rack to cool. Remove the pie from the pan and serve.

Chess Pie

This delicious pie is enriched with egg yolks and has a smooth, silky texture.

Serves 8

Generous 1 cup/175g all-purpose flour
Pinch salt
⅔ stick/75g chilled butter, diced
2 tbsp cold water
1–2 tsp confectioners' sugar, to dust

For the filling:
1 stick/115g butter, softened
Generous 1 cup/225g sugar
Finely grated peel ½ lemon
Pinch salt
3 egg yolks
1 tbsp lemon juice

1. Sift the flour and salt into a bowl. Rub in the butter until the mixture resembles bread crumbs. Sprinkle over the water and mix to a firm dough. Knead briefly, wrap, and chill for 30 minutes.

2. Put a baking sheet in the oven and preheat to 400°F/200°C. Roll out the pastry on a floured surface and line a shallow 9in/23cm tart pan. Prick the base all over then chill for 10 minutes.

3. Line the pie shell with baking parchment and fill with baking beans. Bake for 15 minutes. Remove the parchment and beans, then bake for 5 minutes more. Reduce the temperature to 325°F/160°C.

4. Cream together the butter, sugar, lemon peel, and salt until light and fluffy. Beat in the egg yolks, one at a time, then stir in the lemon juice.

5. Spoon the filling into the pie shell and roughly spread it out. Bake for another 25 to 30 minutes, or until lightly set.

6. Let the pie settle for 10 minutes before removing from the pan. Serve dusted with confectioners' sugar.

Crumb Pie

Serves 6

¾ cup/115g all-purpose flour
Pinch salt
½ stick/50g butter, diced
1 egg yolk
1½ tbsp cold water

For the topping:
¼ cup/40g all-purpose flour
1 cup/75g cake crumbs
1 tsp ground cinnamon
Pinch freshly grated nutmeg
Pinch ground ginger
⅔ stick/75g butter

For the filling:
⅔ cup/150g packed light brown sugar
Scant ⅓ cup/75ml hot water
2 eggs, lightly beaten
½ cup/75g raisins

1. Sift the flour and salt into a bowl. Rub in the butter until the mixture resembles bread crumbs. Mix together the egg yolk and water. Add all but 2 tsp of the egg mixture and mix to a firm dough. Knead until smooth, wrap, and chill for 30 minutes.

2. Preheat the oven to 400°F/200°C. Roll out the pastry on a floured surface and use to line an 8in/20cm tart pan. Prick the base all over, then chill for 15 minutes. Line the pie shell with baking parchment and baking beans. Bake for 15 minutes. Remove the parchment and beans, brush the base with the reserved egg, and bake for 5 minutes more. Reduce the temperature to 325°F/160°C.

3. For the topping, sift the flour into a bowl and stir in the cake crumbs and spices. Rub in the butter until the mixture resembles coarse bread crumbs. Set aside.

4. For the filling, put the sugar, water, and eggs into a bowl set over a pan of simmering water, stirring for 7 to 8 minutes, until the mixture thickens. Sprinkle the raisins over the base of the pie shell, then pour in the filling. Sprinkle over the crumb mixture and bake for 20 to 25 minutes, or until lightly set.

Raspberry and Coconut Pie

*Children will love a slice of this pie
and it's especially good for lunch
boxes or picnics.*

Serves 8

1⅔ cups/250g all-purpose flour
Pinch salt
⅔ stick/75g cold sweet butter, diced
2oz/55g vegetable shortening
2–3 tbsp cold water

For the filling:
1¾ sticks/175g sweet butter
Scant 1 cup/175g sugar
3 eggs, beaten
10oz/275g unsweetened
   shredded coconut
4 tbsp raspberry jelly

1. Sift the flour and salt into a bowl. Rub or
cut in the fat until the mixture resembles
fine bread crumbs. Add 2 tbsp water and
mix to a firm dough, adding a little more
water, if necessary. Turn the dough onto a
lightly floured surface and knead briefly,
until the dough is smooth. Form into a
neat ball, wrap in plastic wrap, and chill
for 20 minutes.

2. Roll out the pastry to line a rectangular
12 x 8in/30 x 20cm loose-bottomed tart
pan. Prick the base with a fork and chill for
10 minutes. Meanwhile, put a baking sheet
in the oven and preheat to 375°F/190°C.

3. To make the filling, beat the butter and
sugar until light and fluffy. Slowly beat in
the eggs and fold in the coconut.

4. Spread the jelly over the pastry base and
spoon the coconut mixture on top, leveling
out the surface.

5. Bake for 35 to 40 minutes. Let cool a
little and cut into slices.

Jefferson Davis Pie

For a Kentucky pie, leave out the spices and nuts and add more dried fruit.

Serves 8–10

Generous 1 cup/175g all-purpose flour
1 stick/115g firm sweet butter, diced
2 tsp sugar
1 egg, lightly beaten

For the filling:
1 stick/115g sweet butter
1 cup/225g packed light brown sugar
1 tsp ground cinnamon
½ tsp ground allspice
Pinch freshly grated nutmeg
4 egg yolks
2 tbsp all-purpose flour
1 cup/240ml heavy cream
½ cup/75g raisins
½ cup/75g chopped dates
½ cup/75g chopped pecan nuts

1. Sift the flour into a bowl and rub or cut in the butter until the mixture resembles bread crumbs. Stir in the sugar, add all but 2 tsp of the egg, and mix to a firm dough. Knead, wrap, and chill for 30 minutes.

2. Put a baking sheet in the oven and preheat to 400°F/200°C. Roll out the pastry on a floured surface and use to line a shallow 9in/23cm tart pan. Prick the base all over with a fork then chill for 10 minutes.

3. Line the pie shell with baking parchment and baking beans. Bake blind for 15 minutes. Remove the parchment and beans and bake for 5 minutes more. Reduce the temperature to 325°F/160°C.

4. For the filling, cream together the butter, sugar, and spices until light then beat in the egg yolks, one at a time. Sift over the flour and beat in, then stir in the cream, raisins, dates, and nuts.

5. Spoon the filling into the pie shell and bake for 30 minutes, or until lightly set. Let settle for 10 minutes, then serve warm.

Apricot Meringue Pie

Serves 6–8

1 cup/150g all-purpose flour
Pinch salt
2 tbsp sugar
⅔ stick/75g chilled butter
2 egg yolks
2 tsp cold water
½ tsp vanilla extract

For the filling:
2lb/900g firm ripe apricots peeled,
   halved, and pitted
Juice ½ lemon
3–4 tbsp sugar, to taste
1 tbsp cornstarch, sifted
¼ tsp ground cinnamon

For the meringue topping:
3 egg whites
¼ tsp cream of tartar
¾ cup/150g sugar

1. Sift the flour, salt, and sugar into a
bowl. Rub in the butter until the mixture
resembles bread crumbs. Beat the egg yolks,
water, and vanilla extract together and reserve
2 tsp of the mixture. Stir the rest into the dry
ingredients to form a soft dough. Wrap and chill
for 30 minutes.

2. Put a baking sheet in the oven and preheat
to 400°F/200°C. Roll out the pastry on a floured
surface and line a shallow 9in/23cm tart pan.
Prick the base all over then chill for 10 minutes.
Line the pie shell with baking parchment and
baking beans. Bake for 15 minutes. Remove the
parchment and beans, brush the base of the pie
shell with the reserved egg, and bake for 5
minutes. Reduce the temperature to 325°F/160°C

3. Put the apricots in a bowl. Squeeze over the
lemon juice. Mix together the sugar, cornstarch,
and cinnamon. Sprinkle over the apricots and
toss to coat in the mixture. Beat the egg white
and cream of tartar in a bowl until stiff peaks
form. Beat in the sugar, gradually, until the
meringue is thick and glossy. Tip the apricots
into the pie shell and spread out. Spoon over
the meringue and bake for 25 minutes.

Blacksmith Pie

Serves 6–8

⅔ stick/75g butter, melted
6oz/175g chocolate-covered
   Graham crackers, crushed
1 tsp unsweetened cocoa powder,

For the filling:
3 tbsp cornstarch
1 cup/200g sugar, plus 2 tbsp
1 cup/240ml milk
½ cup/120ml light cream
2 egg yolks
1 egg
½ cup/75g semisweet chocolate chips
1¼ cups/300ml heavy cream
1 tsp vanilla extract
2 egg whites

1. Line the base of an 8–8½in/20–21cm round loose-bottomed pan with baking parchment. Melt the butter in a pan, then stir in the cracker crumbs and mix together. Press over the base and sides of the pan. Chill while making the filling.

2. Combine the cornstarch, the 2 tbsp of sugar, milk, and light cream in a pan. Stir over a low heat with a whisk until thickened and smooth. Turn off the heat.

3. Beat the egg yolks and egg together. Stir in a spoonful of hot custard, then stir the egg mixture into the rest of the custard in the pan. Slowly bring to a boil, stirring until slightly thickened.

4. Transfer 1 cup/240ml of the hot custard to a bowl. Add the chocolate chips and stir until melted. Spoon into the pie shell, spreading over the base and slightly up the sides. Chill.

5. Cover the remaining custard with dampened baking parchment and let cool. Beat the heavy cream, vanilla extract, and half the sugar until soft peaks form. Beat the egg whites until stiff, then gradually beat in the remaining sugar.

6. Stir the custard until smooth. Fold in the whipped cream and meringue mixture. Pour into the pie shell and chill for at least 1 hour. Dust with cocoa before serving.

Almond Pithiviers

Serves 8

12oz/350g ready-made puff pastry,
    thawed if frozen
1 egg, beaten
1 tbsp confectioners' sugar, to dust

For the filling:
1 cup/240ml milk
1 tsp vanilla extract
3 egg yolks
¼ cup/50g sugar
1 heaping tbsp cornstarch
Scant 1¼ sticks/120g sweet butter,
    softened
Scant ½ cup/100g sugar
Scant 1⅔ cups/120g ground almonds

1. Preheat the oven to 400°F/200°C. For the filling, put the milk and vanilla in a pan and slowly bring to a boil. Mix the egg yolks, sugar, and cornstarch together. Pour the milk over the egg yolk mixture and stir.

2. Return the mixture to the pan and cook over low heat, stirring for 1 minute, or until thick. Remove from the heat and wrap. Let cool.

3. Beat the butter and sugar together until light and fluffy. Stir in the ground almonds then fold in the cold custard.

4. Divide the pastry into 2 pieces. Roll out one piece to ⅛in/3mm thick and cut out a 10in/25cm circle. Place on a nonstick baking sheet and spread the almond mixture over the pastry, leaving a 1in/2.5cm margin around the edge. Brush the edge with beaten egg.

5. Roll out the remaining pastry to the same thickness and cut an 11in/28cm circle. Lay it over the almond-topped pastry and press down to seal the edges. Chill for 30 minutes.

6. Brush the surface with beaten egg and score the top in a diamond pattern. Bake for 35 to 40 minutes until golden. Let stand for 5 minutes before dusting with confectioners' sugar and serving.

CHAPTER THREE

. . . .

Rich and Creamy Pies

Mississippi Mud Pie

*Although named after the rich mud
that lines the banks and bed of the
Mississippi, this pie tastes delicious
and is a much-loved classic!*

Serves 8

⅔ stick/75g butter
1 cup/150g all-purpose flour
½ cup/60g chopped walnuts
2 tbsp iced water
Cocoa powder and
   chopped nuts, to decorate

For the filling:
1 cup/115g confectioners' sugar
1 (8oz/225g) package cream
   cheese, softened
2 cups/475ml heavy cream, whipped
1 (6oz/175g) package instant
   chocolate pudding mix
4 cups milk
1 heaping tsp unsweetened
   cocoa powder

1. Put a baking sheet in the oven and preheat to 350°F/180°C. Soften the butter then blend with the flour, rubbing together lightly with your fingertips until it is the consistency of bread crumbs. Add the walnuts and water.

2. Press the mixture into a 9in/23cm pie plate, and bake for 12 to 15 minutes. Remove from the oven and let cool.

3. In a separate bowl, combine the confectioners' sugar, cream cheese, and 1 cup/240ml of the cream. Gently spread the mixture over the first cooked layer. Chill while you prepare the pudding mix with the milk in another bowl, according to the instructions on the package. Mix in the cocoa.

4. Remove the pie from the refrigerator and spread the chocolate pudding mix over the second layer. Top with whipped cream, dust with a fine layer of cocoa powder, and sprinkle with chopped nuts. Refrigerate for another 4 hours before serving.

Bourbon Pie

Serves 8–10

Generous 1 cup/175g all-purpose flour
Pinch salt
7 tbsp/90g chilled butter, diced
2 tbsp cold water

For the filling:
$\frac{1}{3}$ cup/75g packed dark brown sugar
$\frac{2}{3}$ stick/75g butter, softened
3 eggs, lightly beaten
1 tsp cornstarch
$\frac{2}{3}$ cup/160ml light corn syrup
$\frac{2}{3}$ cup/160ml maple syrup
4 tbsp Bourbon
1 tsp vanilla extract
1$\frac{3}{4}$ cups/175g chopped pecans or walnuts

For the Bourbon cream:
1 cup/240ml heavy cream
2 tbsp Bourbon
1 tbsp dark brown sugar

1. Sift the flour and salt into a bowl. Rub in the butter until the mixture resembles bread crumbs. Sprinkle over the water and mix to a firm dough. Knead until smooth, wrap, and chill for 30 minutes.

2. Put a baking sheet in the oven and preheat to 400°F/200°C. Roll out the pastry on a floured surface and line a 9in/23cm tart pan. Prick the base and chill for 10 minutes.

3. Line the pie shell with baking parchment and baking beans. Bake for 15 minutes. Remove the parchment and beans, brush the base with 1 tsp beaten egg from the filling, and bake for 5 minutes more. Reduce the temperature to 350°F/180°C.

4. Beat the sugar and butter until creamy. Gradually beat in the eggs and cornstarch. Stir in the syrups, Bourbon, vanilla, and nuts. Pour into the pie shell and bake for 35 to 40 minutes, or until the filling is just set.

5. For the cream, whip the cream, Bourbon, and sugar until soft peaks form. Serve the pie warm with the cream.

Chocolate Cream Pie

A rich, dark chocolate filling is poured into a buttery pastry shell and chilled until set. Swirls of cream and curls of chocolate make this pie truly decadent.

Serves 6–8

Generous 1 cup/175g all-purpose flour
2 tbsp sugar
1 stick/115g butter, diced
1 egg yolk
2–3 tsp cold water
Chocolate curls, to decorate

For the filling:
Generous ½ cup/50g cornstarch
Scant ½ cup/90g sugar
⅔ cup/160ml light cream
Scant 1¼ cups/275ml milk
3½oz/90g semisweet chocolate, broken into pieces
2 egg yolks
2 tbsp butter

For the topping:
1 cup/240ml heavy cream
½ tsp vanilla extract
2 tsp confectioners' sugar, sifted

1. Sift the flour and sugar into a bowl. Rub in the butter until the mixture resembles fine bread crumbs. Mix together the egg yolk and 2 tsp water and sprinkle over the dry ingredients. Mix to a firm dough, adding the extra water if needed. Lightly knead, then wrap in plastic wrap and chill for 30 minutes.

2. Put a baking sheet in the oven and preheat to 400°F/200°C. Roll out the pastry on a lightly floured surface and use to line a shallow 8-9in/20-23cm pie plate. Chill for 10 minutes.

3. Line the pie shell with baking parchment and baking beans. Bake blind for 15 minutes. Remove the parchment and beans and cook for another 8 to 10 minutes, or until the pie shell is golden and crisp. Remove from the oven and let cool on a wire rack.

4. To make the filling, mix the cornstarch and sugar in a nonstick pan. Gradually blend in the cream, and then stir in the milk and chocolate. Gently heat, stirring constantly until the chocolate melts and the mixture thickens and boils. Remove from the heat.

5. Beat the egg yolks in a small bowl. Stir in a few spoonfuls of the chocolate mixture, one at a time, and then pour the egg mixture back into the chocolate mixture in the pan, stirring constantly. Cook and continue to stir for another 1 minute, but do not boil. Remove from the heat and stir in the butter. Cool for a few minutes, then pour into the pie shell. To prevent a skin forming, press a circle of dampened baking parchment onto the surface of the filling. Let cool, then chill for 2 hours. Remove the baking parchment.

6. For the topping, pour the cream into a chilled bowl. Stir in the vanilla extract and sugar. Whip until the cream forms soft peaks, and then spoon into a pastry bag with a large star nozzle, and pipe a lattice pattern on top of the pie. Scatter with chocolate curls and serve.

Cook's Tip:
To make thick chocolate curls, melt 6oz/175g semisweet chocolate with 2 tbsp pure white vegetable fat (which stops the chocolate hardening completely), stirring until smooth. Pour into a small rectangular pan lined with baking parchment, to produce a thick block. Chill until set. Let the block come to room temperature, then hold it over a plate and pull the blade of a swivel-bladed peeler firmly along the edge of the chocolate to make the curls.

Black-bottom Cream Pie

This luxurious chocolate pastry cream pie hails from the Deep South.

Serves 8

¾ cup/115g all-purpose flour
3 tbsp unsweetened cocoa powder
2 tbsp confectioners' sugar
⅔ stick/75g chilled butter, diced
1 egg yolk
1 tbsp cold water
Grated chocolate, to decorate

For the filling:
4 egg yolks
¼ cup/50g sugar
4 tsp cornstarch
1¾ cups/400ml milk
2oz/55g semisweet chocolate
1 tbsp dark rum

For the topping:
1½ tsp powdered gelatin
2 tbsp cold water

½ cup/120ml heavy cream
2 tbsp dark rum
3 egg whites
⅓ cup/40g confectioners' sugar, sifted
½ tsp cream of tartar

1. Sift the flour, cocoa, and sugar into a bowl. Rub in the butter until the mixture resembles bread crumbs. Mix the egg yolk and water, add to the dry ingredients, and mix to a firm dough. Knead, wrap, and chill for 30 minutes.

2. Put a baking sheet in the oven and preheat to 400°F/200°C. Sift a little extra flour and cocoa onto a surface, roll out the pastry, and line a greased 9in/23cm pie pan. Prick the base all over, line with foil and baking beans, and bake for 15 minutes. Remove the foil and beans, and bake for 10 minutes more. Let cool.

3. For the filling, beat the egg yolks, sugar, and cornstarch together. Bring the milk to a boil, then pour over the egg mixture, beating. Return to the pan and stir over low heat until thickened. Remove from the heat and stir in the chocolate until melted, followed by the rum. Spoon the mixture into the pie shell. Let cool.

4. For the topping, sprinkle the gelatin over the water in a bowl and let soak for 5 minutes. Set the bowl over a pan of barely simmering water and stir until dissolved. Let cool, but not set. Whip the cream until soft peaks form, then slowly beat in the gelatin and rum. Chill for 30 minutes, or until starting to thicken, but not set.

5. Beat the egg whites until stiff, then beat in the confectioners' sugar, a tablespoon at a time, with the cream of tartar. Fold into the cream mixture, then spoon it on top of the pie. Chill in the refrigerator until set, then decorate with grated chocolate.

Coconut Cream Pie

Serves 8

¾ cup/115g all-purpose flour
5 tbsp/65g sweet butter, diced
1 tbsp sugar
½ cup/40g shredded coconut
1 egg yolk
2 tbsp cold water
Toasted shredded coconut, to decorate
2 tsp confectioners' sugar, to dust

For the filling:
3 eggs, lightly beaten
½ cup/100g sugar
2 tbsp/15g cornstarch
1 (13–14oz/400ml) can coconut milk
⅔ cup/160ml heavy cream

1. Sift the flour into a bowl. Rub in the butter until the mixture resembles bread crumbs. Stir in the sugar and coconut. Mix the egg yolk and water together, sprinkle over the dry ingredients, and mix to a firm dough. Knead, wrap, and chill for 30 minutes.

2. Preheat the oven to 400°F/200°C. Roll out the pastry on a floured surface and line a 9in/23cm tart pan. Prick the base, then chill for 15 minutes.

3. Line the pie shell with baking parchment and baking beans. Bake for 15 minutes. Remove the parchment and beans, brush the base with 1 tsp of egg from the filling, and cook for 5 minutes more. Reduce the temperature to 300°F/150°C.

4. For the filling, beat the eggs and sugar together in a bowl. Blend the cornstarch with a little of the coconut milk in a pan, then stir in the remaining coconut milk. Bring to a boil, stirring constantly until thickened. Remove from the heat and stir in the cream. Pour over the egg mixture, beating constantly.

5. Pour the filling into the pie shell. Bake for 30 to 35 minutes, or until just set. Let cool on a wire rack, then remove from the pan and chill for several hours before serving. Decorate with toasted coconut and confectioners' sugar.

Frangipani Cream Pie

*Delicious frangipani is a thick
mixture of ground almonds, blended
together with butter, eggs, and
sometimes a little flour.*

Serves 8

7oz/200g puff pastry, thawed if frozen
1 cup/115g ground almonds
Generous ½ cup/115g sugar
½ stick/50g butter, softened
3 eggs, lightly beaten
1 tbsp all-purpose flour
3 tbsp apricot jelly

For the topping:
⅔ cup/160ml heavy cream
2 tbsp confectioners' sugar, sifted
2 drops almond extract

1. Roll out the pastry on a lightly floured
surface, and use to line a 9in/23cm pie
plate. Prick the base all over with a fork
and knock up the edge of the pastry with
the back of a knife. Chill in the refrigerator
while making the filling.

2. Put a baking sheet in the oven and
preheat to 400°F/200°C. Put the almonds,
sugar, and butter in a bowl and beat together.
Gradually beat in the eggs a little at a time.
Sift over the flour and stir in, together with
1 tbsp of the cream from the topping.

3. Spread the jelly over the base of the pie
shell, and then spoon the filling over the
jelly and spread it out evenly. Bake for 30
minutes, or until the filling is set and the
pastry browned and crisp.

4. Chill the pie in the refrigerator for 1 hour.
To make the topping, pour the cream into
a chilled bowl and stir in 1 tbsp of the
confectioners' sugar and the almond extract.
Whip until soft peaks form, and then spoon
into a pastry bag and pipe swirls of cream
around the edge of the pie. Dust with
confectioners' sugar before serving.

Raisin Cheese Pie

Serves 8

½ cup/75g all-purpose flour
½ cup/75g self-rising flour
7 tbsp/90g butter, diced
2 tbsp cold water

For the filling:
½ cup/75g seedless raisins
2 tbsp dark rum or orange juice
1 cup/225g curd or ricotta cheese
2 eggs, separated
¼ cup/50g sugar
1 tsp vanilla extract
⅔ cup/160ml heavy cream

1. Sift the flours into a bowl. Rub in the butter until the mixture resembles bread crumbs. Sprinkle the water over the dry ingredients and mix to a firm dough. Knead, wrap, and chill for 30 minutes.

2. For the filling, put the raisins in a small bowl with the rum and let soak.

3. Preheat the oven to 400°F/200°C. Roll out the pastry on a floured surface and line a 9in/23cm plain tart pan. Prick the base all over then chill for 15 minutes.

4. Line the pie shell with baking parchment and baking beans. Bake blind for 10 minutes. Remove the parchment and beans and bake for 5 minutes more. Reduce the oven temperature to 300°F/150°C.

5. Beat the cheese until soft, then stir in the raisins. Beat the egg yolks, sugar, and vanilla extract until pale. Still beating, add the cream, and continue beating until stiff. Fold into the raisin mixture.

6. Beat the egg whites until stiff, then fold into the cheese mixture. Spoon into the pie shell, and bake for 45 minutes to 1 hour, or until the filling is just set. Turn off the heat and let cool in the oven for 15 minutes. Let cool in the pan, then chill overnight before serving.

Caramel Cream Pie

A crisp shortcrust pastry case is ideal for this smooth, caramel filling.

Serves 8

Generous 1 cup/175g all-purpose flour
Pinch salt
7 tbsp/90g chilled butter, diced
2 tbsp water

For the filling:
Generous ½ cup/115g sugar
⅓ cup/80ml hot water
1¾ cups/400ml milk
½ stick/50g butter
¼ cup/40g all-purpose flour
⅔ cup/150g packed light brown sugar
2 eggs, lightly beaten
3 tbsp heavy cream

For the topping:
1 cup/240ml heavy cream
1 tbsp light brown sugar
Pinch cream of tartar

1. Sift the flour and salt into a bowl, and rub in the butter until the mixture resembles fine bread crumbs. Sprinkle over the water and mix to a firm dough, adding a little extra water if necessary. Knead briefly, then wrap in plastic wrap and chill for 30 minutes.

2. Put a baking sheet in the oven and preheat to 400°F/200°C. Roll out the pastry on a floured surface and use to line a 9in/23cm tart pan. Prick the base all over, with a fork. Chill for 10 minutes.

3. Line the pie shell with baking parchment and baking beans. Bake blind for 15 minutes. Remove the parchment and beans, brush the base with 1 tsp beaten egg from the filling, and bake for 5 minutes more. Reduce the temperature to 325°F/160°C.

4. To make the filling, put the sugar and 2 tbsp water in a small heavy pan over low heat. When the sugar has dissolved, increase the heat and cook, without stirring, until it

is a dark golden color. Remove from the heat
and, when the bubbles have subsided, pour
in the hot water, taking care, as the mixture
will splutter. If necessary, reheat to dissolve
the caramel. Cool for a few minutes, and
then stir in the milk.

5. In another pan, melt the butter, then
remove from the heat and stir in the flour
and brown sugar. Stir in the eggs, followed
by the caramel mixture and cream. Cook
over low heat, stirring constantly until the
mixture thickens slightly, but do not boil.

6. Pour the filling into the pie shell
and bake for 20 minutes, or until lightly set;
the filling will firm up as it cools. Remove
and leave on a wire rack until completely
cold. Chill for 2 hours.

7. For the topping, pour the cream into
a chilled bowl and stir in the sugar and
cream of tartar. Whip until soft peaks
form, then spread over the filling.

Custard Pie

This smooth and creamy custard pie, scented with pure vanilla, should still be slightly wobbly when you remove it from the oven, as it will continue to firm up as it cools. It's especially good served with fresh fruit such as raspberries or blueberries.

Serves 6

Generous 1 cup/175g all-purpose flour
1 stick/115g butter
2 tbsp sugar
1 egg yolk
2–3 tsp cold water
Fresh fruit, to serve

For the filling:
2 eggs, lightly beaten
2 egg yolks
Scant ¼ cup/40g sugar
Scant 2 cups/450ml light cream
½ vanilla bean, split

1. Sift the flour into a bowl, then rub or cut in the butter until the mixture resembles fine bread crumbs. Stir in the sugar. Mix the egg yolk and 2 tbsp of the water together, and then sprinkle over the dry ingredients. Mix to a firm dough, adding more water if needed. Knead lightly, wrap in plastic wrap, and chill for 30 minutes.

2. Put a baking sheet in the oven and preheat to 400°F/200°C. Roll out the pastry on a lightly floured surface and use to line an 1½in/4cm deep, 8in/20cm loose-bottomed fluted tart pan. Let chill for 10 minutes.

3. Line the pie shell with baking parchment and baking beans. Bake blind for 15 minutes. Remove the parchment and beans, brush the base with 1 tsp beaten egg from the filling, and cook for 5 minutes more. Reduce the temperature to 300°F/150°C.

4. To make the filling, beat the remaining eggs, egg yolks, and sugar together in a bowl. Pour the cream into a pan, add the vanilla bean, and gently heat until the cream reaches boiling point. Pour onto the egg mixture, beating constantly, then strain into the pie shell.

5. Bake the pie for 40 to 45 minutes, or until the center is lightly set. Remove and let cool on a wire rack before removing from the pan. Serve at room temperature or chilled with fresh fruit to accompany.

Key Lime Pie

Greenish-yellow key limes, sometimes known as Mexican limes, are thin-skinned and have a distinctive aroma, which makes them ideal for many uses. Try to get hold of them for this tasty pie.

Serves 6–8

About 35 vanilla wafers or cookies
2–3 tbsp sugar
⅔ stick/75g butter, melted

For the filling:
1 (8oz/225g) can sweetened condensed milk
½ cup/120ml freshly squeezed key lime juice
3 egg yolks
1 cup/240ml heavy cream, whipped, to decorate and serve
Lime peel (optional), to decorate

1. Lightly grease a 9in/23cm pie plate. Put the wafers or cookies in a strong plastic bag and crush with a rolling pin until very fine crumbs form. Alternatively, use a food processor. Mix the crumbs with the sugar and butter.

2. Pour the crumbs into the pie plate and, using the back of a spoon, press them evenly onto the base and side of the plate. Refrigerate until well chilled.

3. To make the filling, beat the condensed milk with the lime juice and egg yolks in a bowl until well blended and thickened. Pour into the crust and chill until set.

4. Decorate with a little whipped cream and lime peel, if you like. Serve with additional whipped cream.

Ice Cream Pie

Vanilla and chocolate ice cream make the best filling for this luscious pie.

Serves 6–8

6oz/175g chocolate chip cookies, crushed
Generous ¾ stick/85g sweet butter, melted

For the filling:
3 cups/750ml vanilla ice cream, slightly softened
3 cups/750ml chocolate ice cream, slightly softened

For the sauce:
5oz/150g milk chocolate, broken into pieces
Scant ¼ stick/25g sweet butter
½ cup/30g light corn syrup
3 tbsp water
1oz/25g finely chopped hazelnuts

1. Mix the crushed cookies with the melted butter and press the mixture into the base and halfway up the sides of an 8in/20cm springform cake pan. Chill in the refrigerator for 20 minutes, or until firm.

2. Pile alternate scoops of vanilla and chocolate ice cream over the cookie base, leaving the top quite rough. Freeze for at least 1 hour, or until the ice cream is firm.

3. Meanwhile, make the sauce. Put the chocolate, butter, and syrup in a bowl with the water and melt over a pan of gently simmering water. Stir until smooth, then remove from the heat and let cool.

4. Toast the chopped hazelnuts under a preheated broiler for 2 to 3 minutes, or until dark golden.

5. Remove the pie from the pan. Pour the sauce over the ice cream and scatter with the hazelnuts. Freeze until ready to serve, or serve at once.

Banoffee Pie

Serves 6–8

1 cup/150g all-purpose flour
1 stick/115g chilled butter, finely diced
¼ cup/50g sugar

For the filling:
1 stick/115g butter
½ cup/115g packed light brown sugar
2 tbsp light corn syrup
1 (7oz/200g) can sweetened
   condensed skim milk
2 medium bananas
1 tbsp lemon juice
⅔ cup/160ml heavy cream
2oz/55g semisweet chocolate,
   coarsely grated, to decorate

1. Sift the flour into a bowl, then rub in the butter until the mixture resembles coarse bread crumbs. Stir in the sugar, then mix to a soft dough. Wrap and chill for 30 minutes.

2. Put a baking sheet in the oven and preheat to 325°F/160°C. Press the pastry into an 8in/20cm loose-bottomed tart pan. Prick the base all over with a fork, then chill for 10 minutes. Line the pie shell with baking parchment and baking beans. Bake blind for 15 minutes. Remove the parchment and beans and cook for 10 minutes more, or until deep golden and crisp. Place on a wire rack to cool.

3. For the filling, put the butter in a pan over low heat. When it starts to melt, add the sugar, syrup, and condensed milk. Heat gently until the sugar has dissolved.

4. Bring to a boil then simmer for 8 to 10 minutes, stirring until a light caramel color. Cool for a few minutes, then pour into the pie shell and let cool completely.

5. Peel the bananas and slice diagonally. Toss the slices in lemon juice, then arrange in concentric circles in the center of the pie. Whip the cream until soft peaks form, then pipe swirls around the edge. Decorate with grated chocolate.

CHAPTER FOUR

. . . .

Open-Faced Dessert Pies

Blueberry Streusel Tart

This has to be the best blueberry recipe there is!

Serves 8

1¼ sticks/125g butter, softened
3 tbsp sugar
1 egg
2 cups/300g all-purpose flour
¼ cup/60ml light cream
½ tsp pure vanilla extract
2 tbsp finely ground almonds
2 tbsp soft white bread crumbs
Plain yogurt, to serve

For the filling:
1lb 9oz/700g blueberries
½ cup/100g sugar
5 tbsp soft white bread crumbs
3 tbsp slivered almonds
2 tbsp light brown sugar
½ tsp ground cinnamon

1. Put a baking sheet in the oven and preheat to 400°F/200°C. Grease a 10½in/27cm pan.

2. Beat the butter and sugar together in a bowl. When the mixture is light and fluffy, beat in the egg with a little of the flour. Stir in the remaining flour alternately with the cream and vanilla extract, mixing to a smooth, soft dough. Spoon the dough into the pan, then gently ease it evenly over the base of the pan and up the sides.

3. Mix the ground almonds and bread crumbs together, and sprinkle the mixture evenly over the base of the pie shell.

4. To make the filling, mix the blueberries with the sugar and half the bread crumbs. Spoon the mixture into the pie shell.

5. In a bowl, mix the remaining bread crumbs with the slivered almonds, brown sugar, and cinnamon. Scatter the mixture evenly over the blueberries.

6. Bake for 30 minutes, or until the pastry is cooked and the streusel topping is golden. Serve warm with yogurt.

Linzertorte with a Lattice Top

Serve with heavy cream for the quintessential dessert.

Serves 8

1½ cups/225g all-purpose flour
Pinch salt
⅓ cup/50g ground almonds
1¼ sticks/125g, plus ¼ stick/25g sweet
   butter, diced
4 tbsp golden brown sugar
2 eggs, separated
3–4 tsp cold water
Heavy cream, to serve

For the filling:
1lb/450g fresh raspberries
½ cup/100g sugar
2 tsp cornstarch mixed with 2 tsp
   cold water
1 tbsp fresh lemon juice
Confectioners' sugar, to decorate

1. Mix the flour, salt, and ground almonds in a large bowl. Add the butter, and rub in until the mixture resembles fine bread crumbs. Stir in the golden brown sugar. Mix the egg yolks with the cold water. Add to the pastry and bring the dough together. Knead briefly until smooth. Wrap in plastic wrap and chill for 30 minutes.

2. Put the raspberries and sugar into a pan over low heat. Bring to a boil, stir in the cornstarch mixture, and cook for 2 minutes. Remove from the heat, stir in the lemon juice, and leave until cold.

3. Put a baking sheet in the oven and preheat to 400°F/200°C. Roll out about two-thirds of the pastry. Roll the pastry into a rough circle at least 2in/5cm larger than a deep, loose-bottomed 8in/20cm fluted tart pan. Gently roll the pastry onto the rolling pin, then unroll it over the pan to cover. Carefully press the pastry into the edge of the pan, removing any overhanging pastry

with a knife. Prick the base all over with a
fork. Chill for 20 minutes.

4. Roll the pastry trimmings with the
remaining pastry. Cut into ten long strips,
each ¾in/2cm wide using a zigzag cutter.

5. Spoon the raspberry mixture into the
pie shell. Dampen the edges of the pastry
using the egg white, then lay the strips
over the top of the filling to make a lattice
pattern. Lightly press the edges of the
pastry together, and trim off the excess.

6. Bake for 35 to 40 minutes, or until the
pastry is golden. Let cool for 5 minutes.
Remove from the ring and let stand another
10 to 15 minutes. Dust with confectioners'
sugar, and serve warm cut into wedges
with cream.

Tarte Tatin

A French classic, this upside-down tart looks spectacular and is easy to make.

Serves 8

10oz/275g puff pastry, thawed if frozen
Whipped cream or ice cream, to serve

For the filling:
6 eating apples
1 tbsp lemon juice
Scant 1 stick/100g butter
6 tbsp sugar

1. For the filling, peel, core, and slice the apples into quarters, then use a fork to score the rounded side. Cut each quarter in half widthwise, then toss the pieces in the lemon juice.

2. Melt the butter in a 9in/23cm ovenproof frying pan. Stir in the sugar until it has melted, then remove the pan from the heat.

3. Arrange the apple quarters, scored side down, in concentric circles in the pan, Pack them quite tightly. Put the pan over low heat and cook, without disturbing the apples, for 15 minutes, or until they begin to caramelize.

4. Put a baking sheet in the oven and preheat to 400°F/200°C. Roll out the puff pastry on a lightly floured surface to a circle slightly larger than the top of the frying pan. Wrap it over the rolling pin, then carefully place it on top of the apples in the pan. Carefully tuck the edges inside the pan.

5. Transfer the frying pan to the oven and bake the tart for 20 to 25 minutes, or until the pastry is well risen and golden brown.

6. Let the tart cool for 5 minutes, then ease a knife between the top crust and the pan. Invert a plate on top then carefully turn both pan and plate over together so that the apples are on top. Serve warm, with whipped cream or ice cream.

Fig and Ricotta Tart

This tart has a deliciously buttery shortbread base and is topped with creamy ricotta and fresh figs.

Serves 6–8

Generous 1 cup/175g all-purpose flour
Generous ½ cup/80g ground rice
2 sticks/200g sweet butter
Scant ½ cup/100g sugar

For the filling:
1¼ lb/500g ricotta cheese
¾ cup/75g confectioners' sugar
2 tsp vanilla extract
6 ripe figs, quartered
2 tbsp clear runny honey

1. Preheat the oven to 350°F/180°C. Mix the flour and ground rice together. In a separate bowl, cream the butter and sugar together until light and fluffy. Mix in the flour and ground rice, and bring together to form a ball.

2. Press the pastry into the base of a 9in/23cm loose-bottomed tart pan. Prick with a fork and chill for 20 minutes.

3. Bake for 20 to 25 minutes. Let cool completely then remove from the tart pan.

4. To make the filling, beat the ricotta cheese with the confectioners' sugar and vanilla extract. Spread the mixture over the shortbread base, and arrange the figs over the ricotta. Drizzle with honey just before serving.

Tarte au Citron

Serves 8

1 cup/150g all-purpose flour
Pinch salt
⅔ stick/75g chilled butter
1 tbsp sugar
1 egg yolk
1 tbsp chilled water
Confectioners' sugar, to dust

For the filling:
3 large lemons
5 eggs, lightly beaten
2 tbsp/30g sweet butter, melted
¾ cup/150g sugar

1. Sift the flour and salt into a bowl. Rub in the butter until the mixture resembles bread crumbs. Stir in the sugar. Mix the egg yolk and water together, then sprinkle over the dry mixture and mix to a firm dough. Knead, wrap, and chill for 1 hour.

2. Preheat the oven to 400°F/200°C. Roll out the pastry on a floured surface and line an 8½in/21cm round or 13 x 5½in/33 x 14cm rectangular loose-bottomed pie pan. Prick the base all over with a fork.

3. Line the pie shell with baking parchment and baking beans. Bake for 15 minutes. Remove the parchment and beans, then brush the inside of the pie shell with 2 tsp of the beaten egg from the filling. Bake for 5 minutes more. Reduce the temperature to 250°F/120°C.

4. Grate the peel from the lemons. Squeeze the juice; you will need ¾ cup/180ml. Put the lemon peel and juice in a bowl with the eggs, butter, and sugar. Beat until smooth.

5. Pour the filling into the pie shell and bake for 35 to 45 minutes, or until just set. Transfer the pan to a wire rack and leave for 10 minutes before removing the tart from the pan. Let cool, then chill. Dust with confectioners' sugar before serving.

Pear Tart with Walnuts and Star Anise

Serves 6

1½ cups/225g all-purpose flour
Pinch salt
3 egg yolks
1 stick/115g butter
3 tbsp sugar
Beaten egg, to glaze

For the filling:
¾ cup/150g sugar
Scant 2 cups/425ml water
6 whole star anise
6 whole cloves
7 small, firm just-ripe pears
2 tbsp lemon juice
Large strip pared lemon peel, cut into
    fine shreds
¼ cup/25g walnut halves

1. Sift the flour and salt onto a work surface.
Make a well in the center. Add the egg yolks,
butter, and sugar and using your fingertips,
work these together. Gradually work in the
flour. Knead, wrap, and chill for 1 hour.

2. Put the sugar in a pan with the water and
two star anise. Heat until the sugar dissolves, then
bring to a boil and simmer for 1 minute. Halve
and peel the pears. Scoop out the core, then
brush each half with lemon juice. Add to the
syrup, cover, and simmer for 20 minutes, until
tender, turning occasionally.

3. Preheat the oven to 375°F/190°C. Roll out
the pastry and cut out a 10in/25cm round. Put
on a greased baking sheet and push the edge
of the pastry in slightly to form a thicker pie
edge. Prick the base all over. Re-roll the pastry
trimmings and cut out star shapes with a small
cutter. Arrange around the edge, attaching with
beaten egg. Brush with beaten egg, then bake
for 12 to 15 minutes.

4. Arrange the cooked pears cut-side up in the
pie shell. Add the remaining star anise, cloves,
peel, and walnuts to the syrup. Bring to a rapid
boil for 5 minutes, until thickened. Strain the
syrup, reserve, and scatter the star anise, peel,
and walnuts on top of the pears. Drizzle over
a little syrup and serve hot.

Honey and Mixed Nut Tart

Serves 8

1¼ cups/190g all-purpose flour
Pinch salt
Scant 1 stick/100g cold butter, diced
2–3 tbsp cold water
Heavy cream, to serve

For the filling:
1 stick/100g butter
1 cup/240ml honey
2⅓ cups/275g mixed nuts, such as pecan
nuts, walnuts, hazelnuts, almonds

1. Sift the flour and salt into a bowl. Rub in the butter until the mixture resembles fine bread crumbs. Add 2 tbsp water and mix to a firm dough, adding more water, if needed. Turn the dough onto a lightly floured surface and knead until smooth. Form into a ball, wrap, and chill for 20 minutes.

2. Roll out the pastry on a floured surface into a rough circle at least 2in/5cm larger than a loose-bottomed 9in/23cm fluted tart pan. Prick the base all over with a fork. Chill for 20 minutes. Meanwhile, put a baking sheet in the oven and preheat to 400°F/200°C.

3. Remove the pan from the refrigerator and line with baking parchment. Fill with baking beans and bake blind for 12 minutes, then remove the parchment and beans and bake for 10 minutes more, or until pale golden. Cool on a wire rack. Reduce the oven temperature to 375°F/190°C.

4. Heat the butter and honey gently until melted, then increase the heat and let bubble for 1 to 2 minutes, or until starting to darken. Stir in the nuts and return to simmering point. Let cool slightly.

5. Pour the filling into the pie shell and bake for 5 to 7 minutes, or until the nuts are golden and fragrant and the pastry is browned. Serve warm with cream.

Tarte Fine aux Pommes

Quick and simple to make, this fresh-tasting tart is glazed with apricot jelly and tastes superb served with cream.

Serves 4

12oz/350g puff pastry, thawed if frozen

For the filling:
2 eating apples
1½ tbsp confectioners' sugar
2 tbsp apricot jelly
Cream, to serve

1. Roll the pastry out thinly and cut out a 9in/23cm circle. Transfer to a lightly greased baking sheet. Preheat the oven to 375°F/190°C.

2. Halve the apples and thinly slice lengthwise. Lay on the pastry in concentric circles, overlapping slightly and leaving a ½in/1cm margin around the edge. Dust generously with the confectioners' sugar.

3. Transfer the baking sheet to the oven and bake for 20 to 25 minutes, or until the pastry is risen and golden, and the apples are tender and golden at the edges.

4. Gently heat the apricot jelly in a small pan then press through a strainer to remove any large pieces. While the jelly and tart are both hot, brush the jelly generously over the apple slices to glaze. Let cool slightly and serve warm with cold cream.

Peach Tart

Delicious served with whipped cream flavored with almond liqueur.

Serves 6–8

Generous 1 cup/175g all-purpose flour
Pinch salt
½ stick/50g chilled butter, diced
3 tbsp/45g white vegetable shortening
2 tbsp cold water
2–3 tbsp confectioners' sugar, to dust

For the filling:
8 large firm ripe peaches or nectarines
1 tbsp lemon juice
4 tbsp sugar
1 tbsp cornstarch
½ tsp ground cinnamon
⅓ cup/75g blanched slivered almonds

1. Sift the flour and salt into a bowl and rub in the fat until the mixture resembles bread crumbs. Sprinkle over the water and mix to a firm dough. Knead until smooth, wrap, and chill for 30 minutes.

2. Put a baking sheet in the oven and preheat to 400°F/200°C. Roll out the pastry on a lightly floured surface and use to line a 9in/23cm pie plate. Prick the base all over with a fork, and then chill for 10 minutes.

3. Line the pie shell with baking parchment and baking beans. Bake blind for 15 minutes. Remove the parchment and beans and bake for 5 minutes more. Reduce the temperature to 375°F/190°C.

4. Lower the peaches, one at a time into scalding water for 30 to 40 seconds. Remove with a slotted spoon, plunge into cold water, then peel off the skins. Halve, pit, and thickly slice into a bowl. Sprinkle with lemon juice, then sprinkle with a mixture of sugar, cornstarch, and cinnamon. Toss to coat, then transfer to the pie shell.

5. Bake for 20 minutes, then scatter with the almonds. Return to the oven for a further 5 to 10 minutes. Dust with confectioners' sugar before serving.

Orange Chiffon Pie

In the 1950s, ready-prepared frozen pie shells began appearing in supermarkets, and their chiffon fillings were quickly made from instant "Jell-O" packaged desserts. They were a true convenience dessert. However, making a chiffon pie from scratch is almost as quick and easy, as it needs no cooking at all.

Serves 6–8

18–20 Graham crackers, finely crushed
½ stick/50g butter, melted
2 tbsp superfine sugar (optional)
Julienne strips of orange peel, simmered in water until tender, to decorate
Whipped cream, to serve

For the filling:
¼ cup/60ml cold water
1 package or 1 tbsp gelatin
4 eggs, separated
Generous 1¼ cups/275g superfine sugar

Grated peel of 1 orange
½ cup/120ml freshly squeezed orange juice
¼ tsp cream of tartar

1. Combine the crushed crackers, melted butter, and the sugar, if using, in a large bowl. Pour into a 9in/23cm pie dish and, using an 8in/20cm pie dish, press the crumbs firmly against the base and side of the larger pan. Alternatively, use the back of a tablespoon to press the crumbs evenly against the base and side of the dish. Chill until firm.

2. For the filling, pour the water into a coffee cup or small bowl, sprinkle over the gelatin, and let stand for 10 minutes. Set the cup in a pan of just simmering water and heat gently for 5 minutes, stirring until the gelatin has completely dissolved.

3. Using an electric mixer, beat the egg yolks in a large heatproof bowl for 1 to

2 minutes, or until light and fluffy. Gradually beat in half the sugar, the grated orange peel, and the juice. Set the bowl over a pan of just simmering water (the base of the bowl should just touch the water). Cook, stirring constantly, for 8 to 10 minutes, or until the mixture thickens and coats the back of a wooden spoon.

4. Remove the bowl from the water, stir in the gelatin mixture, and cool this custard, stirring occasionally. If you like, set the custard over a bowl of cold water to cool quickly, but do not allow it to set.

5. Using clean beaters, beat the egg whites and cream of tartar in a bowl until fluffy. Continue beating until soft peaks form. Gradually beat in the remaining sugar until the whites are stiff and glossy.

6. Beat a spoonful of the whites into the cooled custard then pour the custard mixture over the whites and fold together until the mixtures are just blended. Do not overwork the mixture—it does not matter if a few lumps of white remain. Pour into the crumb crust, mounding the mixture in the center. Chill for 4 to 6 hours, or until set.

7. Decorate with julienne strips of orange peel and serve with whipped cream.

Pear and Almond Tart

For a grand finale, this rich, buttery tart is something of a showstopper.

Serves 6–8

Scant 2 cups/275g all-purpose flour
2 tbsp/30g confectioners' sugar, plus
  extra to dust
Generous 3 sticks/350g sweet butter,
  cut into cubes
2 egg yolks
4 tbsp iced water

For the filling:
Generous ¾ cup/175g granulated sugar
1½ cups/175g ground almonds
2 eggs
Few drops almond extract (optional)
8 pear halves (about 1 can)
¼ cup/25g sliced almonds

1. Mix the flour and confectioners' sugar together in a bowl. Rub in half the butter until the mixture resembles fine bread crumbs. Beat the egg yolks with the water.

2. Make a well into the center of the flour and pour in the egg mixture. Gradually bring the mixture together to form a smooth ball of pastry. Wrap and chill for 30 minutes. Meanwhile, put a baking sheet in the oven and preheat to 375°F/190°C.

3. Roll out the pastry to line a 9½in/24cm loose-bottomed tart pan. Line with baking parchment and fill with baking beans. Bake for 20 minutes, or until golden and crisp. Remove the parchment and beans. Reduce the temperature to 350°F/180°C.

4. Cream the remaining butter and the granulated sugar until pale and fluffy then mix in the ground almonds. Gradually beat in the eggs and almond extract, if using. Spoon into the pie shell and level out. Arrange the pears on top. Scatter over the sliced almonds.

5. Bake for 55 to 60 minutes. Let cool for 10 minutes, and dust with confectioners' sugar (optional) before serving.

· · · · · · · · · ·

CHAPTER FIVE

Festive and Celebration Pies

Pumpkin Pie

Serves 6–8

2⅓ cups/350g flour
Pinch salt
1½ sticks/175g butter
4–5 tbsp water
Light cream, to serve

For the filling:
2lb/900g pumpkin to yield 1½lb/675g
   pumpkin pulp, flesh cut into
   2in/5cm pieces
2 eggs, beaten
Generous ⅓ cup/90g brown sugar
1 cup/240ml light corn syrup
1 cup/240ml heavy cream
2 tsp ground cinnamon
1 tsp ground ginger
½ tsp freshly grated nutmeg
1 tsp vanilla extract

1. Sift the flour and salt into a bowl. Rub in the butter until the mixture resembles bread crumbs. Add 4 tbsp water and mix to a firm dough, adding more water, if necessary. Knead until smooth. Wrap in plastic wrap and chill for 20 minutes.

2. Roll out the pastry into a rough circle at least 2in/5cm larger than a loose-bottomed 12in/30cm fluted tart pan. Line the tart pan and trim off any excess pastry. Prick the base all over. Chill for 20 minutes. Meanwhile, put a baking sheet in the oven and preheat to 400°F/200°C.

3. Line the pie shell with baking parchment and fill with baking beans. Bake for 20 minutes. Remove the parchment and beans. Reduce the temperature to 375°F/190°C. Put the pumpkin in a pan and cover with water. Bring to a boil, then simmer for 15 minutes, until tender. Drain the pumpkin, cool, and purée, then spoon into a large bowl.

4. Add the eggs, sugar, syrup, and cream to the pumpkin purée and mix. Stir in the spices and vanilla extract. Spoon the filling into the pie shell and bake for 30 to 35 minutes, or until the filling is set. Serve warm with cream.

Sweet Potato Pie

Serves 6–8

Generous 1 cup/175g all-purpose flour
Pinch salt
7 tbsp/90g chilled butter, diced
2 tbsp cold water
Cream, to serve

For the filling:
1lb 9oz/700g sweet potatoes, peeled
1 cup/240ml light cream
2 eggs, lightly beaten
½ stick/50g butter, softened
¼ cup/50g packed light brown sugar
½ tsp ground cinnamon
½ tsp ground ginger
¼ tsp freshly grated nutmeg
1 tsp vanilla extract

1. Sift the flour and salt into a bowl. Rub in the butter until the mixture resembles fine bread crumbs. Sprinkle over the water and mix to a dough. Knead, wrap, and chill for 30 minutes.

2. Roll out the pastry on a floured surface and line a 9in/23cm tart pan. Prick the base all over then chill for 10 minutes.

3. Put a baking sheet in the oven and preheat to 400°F/200°C. Cut the sweet potatoes into large chunks. Put them in a nonstick roasting pan, cover with foil, and roast for 30 minutes, or until soft. Remove, and while warm, mash them in a bowl until very smooth with a few spoonfuls of the cream. About halfway through the sweet potatoes' cooking time, line the pie shell with baking parchment and baking beans. Bake for 15 minutes, remove the parchment and beans, brush with 1 tsp beaten egg from the filling and bake for 5 minutes more. Reduce the temperature to 350°F/180°C.

4. Cream together the butter and sugar until light. Gradually beat in the eggs, then stir in the spices. Stir the remaining cream into the mashed sweet potato, and then stir the two mixtures together. Spoon the filling into the pie shell. Bake for 40 to 45 minutes, or until lightly browned. Serve with cream.

Georgia Pecan Pie

Melt-in-the-mouth pastry contains a rich nutty filling for this traditional pie.

Serves 8–10

1½ cups/225g all-purpose flour
⅓ cup/75g cream cheese, softened
1¼ sticks/125g butter, softened
2 tbsp sugar

For the filling:
3–3½ cups/300–350g pecan halves
3 eggs, lightly beaten
1 cup/225g packed dark brown sugar
½ cup/120ml light corn syrup
Grated peel and juice ½ lemon
½ stick/50g butter, melted and cooled
2 tsp vanilla extract

1. Sift the flour into a large bowl. Add the cream cheese, butter, and sugar and, using a pastry cutter or your fingertips, cut into the flour until the mixture resembles fine bread crumbs. Pour into a 9in/23cm pie plate and press onto the base and up the side, making the edge even with the lip of the pan. Alternatively, form the dough into a ball; flatten, wrap, and chill for 1 hour. Roll out on a floured surface and line the pie plate, leaving a ¼in/5mm stand-up edge. Chill.

2. Put a baking sheet in the oven and preheat to 350°F/180°C. To make the filling, pick out 1 cup/100g perfect pecan halves and set aside. Coarsely chop the remaining nuts.

3. Whisk the eggs and brown sugar until light and foamy. Beat in the syrup, lemon peel and juice, melted butter, and vanilla extract. Stir in the chopped pecans and pour into the pie plate. Carefully arrange the reserved pecans in circles on the top.

4. Bake for 45 minutes, or until the filling is puffed and set, and the pecans are colored. Cool to room temperature before serving.

Apple Strudel

Add dried fruits or toasted nuts to the filling of this classic apple dessert.

Serves 8

6 large sheets of phyllo pastry, about
   2oz/55g, thawed if frozen
½ stick/50g butter, melted
2 tbsp confectioners' sugar, to dust
Sour cream or crème fraîche, to serve

For the filling:
1lb 6oz/650g (about 7) eating apples
½ cup/75g raisins
Grated peel and juice ½ lemon
½ cup/25g fresh white bread crumbs
3 tbsp sugar
½ tsp ground cinnamon

1. Remove the phyllo pastry from the refrigerator and leave, still in its wrapping, at room temperature for 20 minutes.

2. Meanwhile, peel, core, and thinly slice the apples. Put them in a bowl with the raisins and lemon peel. Sprinkle with the lemon juice and toss to coat. Add the bread crumbs, sugar, and cinnamon, and mix again.

3. Preheat the oven to 375°F/190°C. Lay one sheet of phyllo pastry on a damp dishtowel, and lightly brush with melted butter. Place a second sheet on top. Continue to layer the phyllo, brushing butter between each sheet.

4. Spoon the apple mixture over the phyllo pastry leaving a 1in/2.5cm margin around the edges. Turn in the short pastry edges. With the help of the dishtowel, roll up from a long edge to completely enclose the filling.

5. Transfer the strudel to a greased baking sheet, seam-side down. Brush with butter and bake for 35 to 40 minutes until the apples are soft. If necessary, cover the pastry loosely with foil to prevent overbrowning. Dust with confectioners' sugar and serve hot with sour cream or crème fraîche.

Huckleberry Pie

Serves 6

½ cup/75g all-purpose flour
⅓ cup/50g whole wheat flour
Pinch salt
5 tbsp/65g chilled butter, diced
1 tsp grated orange peel
2 tbsp chilled water
Beaten egg, to glaze
1 tbsp Demerara sugar, to sprinkle
Custard or cream, to serve

For the filling:
7 cups/800g huckleberries
6 tbsp/75g sugar, or to taste
2 tbsp cornstarch, sifted
Juice ½ small orange
1 tbsp/15g butter

1. Sift the flours and salt into a bowl. Add the bran left in the strainer, then rub in the butter until the mixture resembles bread crumbs. Stir in the orange peel, then sprinkle the water over the dry ingredients and mix to a firm dough. Knead, wrap, and chill for 30 minutes.

2. Tip the berries into a large bowl. Mix together the sugar and cornstarch and sprinkle over the berries. Squeeze over the orange juice, then toss together. Let stand for 10 minutes.

3. Preheat the oven to 400°F/200°C. Using an inverted 9in/23cm pie dish as a guide, roll out the pastry on a floured surface until it is 2in/5cm larger all around than the dish. Cut a 1in/2.5cm strip from around the edge. Moisten the rim of the pie dish and position the strip on the rim. Brush with water.

4. Spoon the filling into the dish, mounding it in the center. Dot the top with butter. Place the pastry lid on top, seal, and crimp the edges, and cut a steam vent in the top. Brush with beaten egg and sprinkle with Demerara sugar.

5. Bake for 20 minutes, then reduce the temperature to 350°F/180°C and bake 15 to 25 minutes more or until the pastry is lightly browned and crisp. Serve hot with custard or cream.

Cranberry Pie

This single-crust pie couldn't be simpler—a true celebration of the fine flavor of cranberries and the perfect pie to serve at Thanksgiving.

Serves 6

1½ cups/225g all-purpose flour
Pinch salt
Scant 1 stick/100g butter
2 tbsp sugar, plus extra for topping
1 egg
1–2 tbsp milk

For the filling:
1¼ cups/250g sugar
Finely grated peel and juice of 1 orange
6 cups/675g cranberries

1. Preheat the oven to 400°F/200°C. Mix the flour and salt in a bowl. Rub in the butter until the mixture resembles bread crumbs. Stir in the sugar, then add enough of the egg to make a dough. Wrap and let rest in a cool place for 30 minutes.

2. To make the filling, mix the sugar and the grated orange peel and juice in a bowl. Mix well, then stir in the cranberries. Spoon into a deep, 6 cup/1.5 liter pie dish.

3. Roll out the pastry on a lightly floured surface to fit the top of the dish, adding an extra 1in/2.5cm all around. Cut off a 1in/2.5cm strip from around the edge. Dampen the rim of the pie dish lightly with water and stick the pastry strip in place. Add the milk to any remaining egg yolk, and brush a little of this onto the pastry strip. Put the pastry lid on top, seal, and crimp the edges.

4. Decorate the top of the pie with pastry shapes, if you like. Cut one or two vents to allow the steam to escape, then brush the pie crust with the remaining egg and milk mixture. Sprinkle it with sugar. Bake the pie above the center of the oven for 25 to 35 minutes, or until the pastry is golden and crisp. Sprinkle with more sugar and serve with whipped cream.

Banana Cream Pie

This no-bake pie has a simple pie shell made from crushed vanilla wafers, which is lavishly filled with banana slices and smothered with creamy custard. A whipped cream topping makes it extra special.

Serves 8

2 cups vanilla wafer crumbs
5 tbsp/65g butter, melted

For the filling:
$\frac{1}{3}$ cup/40g cornstarch
Scant $\frac{1}{2}$ cup/90g sugar
Scant 2 cups/450ml milk
1 cup/240ml light cream
2 tbsp/30g butter
3 egg yolks
$\frac{1}{2}$ tsp vanilla extract
3 medium bananas
2 tbsp orange juice

For the topping:
$\frac{2}{3}$ cup/160ml heavy cream
1 tbsp confectioners' sugar, sifted
$\frac{1}{2}$ tsp vanilla extract

1. Mix together the wafer crumbs and butter, and press the mixture evenly over the base and up the sides of an 8-9in/20-23cm pie dish. Chill in the refrigerator while making the filling.

2. In a pan, blend the cornstarch and sugar to a paste with a little of the milk, then stir in the remaining milk and cream. Add the butter and cook over low heat, stirring constantly, until the mixture boils and thickens. Simmer for 1 minute more.

3. Remove the pan from the heat and let cool for 1 minute. Mix the egg yolks in a bowl, then stir in a large spoonful of the custard mixture. Stir the egg mixture into the custard mixture, then stir in the vanilla extract. Return to a very low heat and cook for about 5 minutes until the mixture has thickened slightly. Do not let the custard boil or it may curdle.

4. Peel and slice 2 bananas and toss in the orange juice. Remove them from the juice and use to cover the base of the pie shell. Pour the custard over the bananas. Let cool, then chill for 2 hours.

5. For the topping, whip the cream, confectioners' sugar, and vanilla extract until soft peaks form. Spoon and spread the cream in the center of the pie, leaving a border of custard showing.

6. Peel and slice the remaining banana and toss in the orange juice. Arrange in an overlapping circle on top of the cream and serve straight away.

Marshmallow and Chocolate Pie

This sweet pie has a tempting marshmallowy filling and a creamy layer of chocolate that children love!

Serves 8–10

6oz/175g Graham crackers, crushed to fine crumbs
Scant ¾ stick/85g sweet butter, melted

For the filling:
Scant 2⅔ cups/580g cream cheese
Generous ½ cup/120g sugar
1 tsp vanilla extract
3 eggs, beaten
2 egg yolks
4oz/115g mini-marshmallows

For the topping:
1¼ cups/300ml heavy cream
5oz/150g semisweet chocolate, broken into small pieces

1. Mix the Graham crackers with the melted butter and press into the base of a 9in/23cm springform cake pan. Chill for 30 minutes, or until firm. Wrap the outside of the pan in foil. Meanwhile, put a baking sheet in the oven and preheat to 350°F/180°C.

2. To make the filling, mix together the cream cheese, sugar, and vanilla extract in a bowl. Beat in the eggs and egg yolks, and then fold in the marshmallows. Spoon the mixture into the cake pan and level the top.

3. Place the pie in a roasting pan half-full of boiling water and bake for 50 minutes. Let cool, then chill for 2 to 3 hours, or until firm.

4. To make the topping, put the cream in a pan and bring up to boiling point. Remove from the heat and stir in the chocolate until smooth. Let cool for 10 minutes, and then pour the sauce over the pie. Chill until the chocolate has set.

Cherry Strudel

Soft and luscious, this traditional
favorite will have folks dropping by
on all kinds of pretexts.

Serves 8

4 large sheets phyllo pastry, thawed
if frozen
½ stick/50g sweet butter, melted
Confectioners' sugar, to dust

For the filling:
1lb 3oz/550g fresh black cherries,
pitted and halved
¼ cup/40g ground almonds
⅓ cup/90g granulated sugar
1 cup/55g fresh cake crumbs

1. Preheat the oven to 375°F/190°C. To make the filling, place the cherries in a bowl with the ground almonds, granulated sugar, and cake crumbs, and then stir to combine.

2. Cover the phyllo pastry with a damp dishtowel to prevent it drying out. Lay a sheet of the pastry on a large, flat baking sheet and brush with a little melted butter. Lay a second sheet over the top and brush with butter. Repeat this twice more so that you have a rectangle of four sheets of pastry.

3. Spoon the cherry mixture over the top, leaving a gap of 2in/5cm around the edge. Roll up the longest side—like you would a jelly roll. Tuck in the ends and form into a horseshoe shape.

4. Brush the surface of the pastry with more butter and bake for 25 minutes. Dust with confectioners' sugar and serve warm or at room temperature.

Marlborough Pie

This was once a traditional
Thanksgiving dessert and makes
a good alternative to Pumpkin Pie.
The meringue topping is made with
confectioners' sugar and "cooked"
over hot water, so it will hold its shape
for several hours after baking.

Serves 8

Generous 1 cup/175g all-purpose flour
½ tsp ground cinnamon
2 tbsp sugar
1 stick/115g butter, or half butter/half
   white vegetable fat, diced
1 egg yolk
2–3 tsp cold water

For the filling:
350g cooking or tart apples
2 tbsp butter
1 tbsp lemon juice and finely grated peel
   ½ small lemon
¼ cup/50g packed light brown sugar

½ cup/120ml heavy cream
2 egg yolks
⅓ cup/50g raisins
⅓ cup/75g chopped toasted walnuts
   or pecan nuts

For the meringue topping:
3 egg whites
1¾ cups/200g confectioners' sugar, sifted
½ tsp vanilla extract

1. Sift the flour and cinnamon into a bowl.
Stir in the sugar, and then rub or cut in the
butter until the mixture resembles fine
bread crumbs. Mix the egg yolk with 2 tsp
of the water and sprinkle over the dry
ingredients. Mix to a firm dough, adding
the extra water if necessary. Knead briefly,
then wrap in plastic wrap and chill for
30 minutes.

2. Put a baking sheet in the oven and
preheat to 400°F/200°C. Roll out the pastry
on a lightly floured surface and use to line

a 9in/23cm tart pan. Prick the base all over with a fork, and then chill for 10 minutes.

3. Line the pie shell with baking parchment and fill with baking beans. Bake blind for 15 minutes. Remove the parchment and beans, then bake for 5 minutes more. Remove from the oven and reduce the temperature to 325°F/160°C.

4. To make the filling, peel, core, and roughly chop the apples into a pan with the butter and lemon juice. Cook over medium heat until tender and pulpy. Press through a strainer into a pitcher; there should be about 1 cup/240ml purée. Add the lemon peel and sugar, and stir until dissolved. Mix in the cream, followed by the egg yolks.

5. To make the meringue topping, beat the egg whites in a heatproof bowl until peaks form. Set the bowl over a pan of simmering water. Add the sugar and vanilla extract.

Beat until thick. Remove the bowl from the pan and beat for 2 minutes more.

6. Sprinkle the raisins and nuts over the base of the pie shell. Pour the filling into the shell, then carefully spoon and spread the meringue on top. Bake for 30 minutes, or until the meringue is dark golden and crisp.

Cook's Tips:
- Bought apple sauce can be used instead of a fresh apple purée. If sweetened, you should reduce the amount of sugar by half.
- This pie is sometimes served with a whipped cream topping (see Banana Cream Pie, page 102) instead of meringue, allowing the pie to be made the day before and served chilled.

Boston Cream Pie

This well-known dessert is really a layered cake, but the creamy custard filling and its appearance is very pie-like. Fresh fruit, such as a few raspberries or quartered strawberries, can be added to the filling, if you like.

Serves 8

5 eggs
¾ cup/150g sugar
1 cup/150g all-purpose flour
1 tbsp confectioners' sugar, to dust

For the filling:
4 egg yolks
¼ cup/50g sugar
4 tbsp cornstarch
2 tsp vanilla extract
Scant 2 cups/450ml milk
1¼ cups/300ml heavy cream

1. Preheat the oven to 400°F/200°C. Grease and line the bases of a 9in/23cm springform cake pan and a 10½ x 6½in/26 x 17cm shallow rectangular pan with baking parchment.

2. Put the eggs and sugar in a large heatproof bowl set over a pan of barely simmering water, and whisk until the mixture is pale and thick and holds a trail. Remove from the heat and whisk for 3 to 4 minutes more, or until very light.

3. Sift the flour over the mixture and carefully fold in with a metal spoon. Spoon a very thin layer of the batter over the base of the rectangular pan to a depth slightly thicker than ¼in/5mm. Pour and scrape the rest of the batter into the round pan.

4. Bake both cakes for 12 to 15 minutes, or until light golden and firm; the cakes should spring back when lightly pressed with a finger. Let cool in the tins for 5 minutes, then turn out onto wire racks.

5. To make the filling, beat the egg yolks, sugar, cornstarch, vanilla extract, and 2 tbsp of the milk together in a bowl. Heat the remaining milk in a pan to boiling point. Pour over the egg mixture, beating, then return to the pan and heat gently, stirring until thickened, but do not boil. Pour back into the bowl and cover with a piece of damp baking parchment. Let cool.

6. Cut the round sponge horizontally into two layers and fit one back into the cleaned pan, cut-side up. Trim the edges from the rectangular sponge, then cut into 1¼in/3cm wide strips. Fit these around the side of the pan to make a shell.

7. Whip the cream in a chilled bowl until thick. Stir the cooled custard, and then fold in the cream. Pour into the sponge shell and level the surface. Lay the second sponge on top, cut-side up. Chill in the refrigerator overnight. To serve, invert the sponge on a flat plate or board and remove from the pan. Dust with confectioners' sugar before serving.

Index

Glossary

US:UK terms are given below for foods that have different names in the UK:

U.S.	British	U.S.	British
all-purpose flour	plain flour	packed brown sugar	muscovado sugar
almond extract	almond essence	peel	zest
baking soda	bicarbonate of soda	plastic wrap	clingfilm
beat	whisk	self-rising flour	self-raising flour
confectioners' sugar	icing sugar	semisweet chocolate	plain chocolate
cornstarch	cornflour	shredded coconut	desiccated coconut
Graham crackers	digestive biscuits	sugar	caster sugar
jelly	jam	sweet butter	unsalted butter
light corn syrup	golden syrup	vanilla bean	vanilla pod
light cream	single cream	whole wheat flour	wholemeal flour

Picture Credits

Page 7 © Kieran Scott/Anthony Blake Photo Library.
Pages 15, 18, 22, 37, 49, 62, 69, 75, 79, 82, 87, 90, 95, 100 © Cephas/Stockfood.
Page 27 © Martin Brigdale/Anthony Blake Photo Library.
Page 42 © Condé Nast Archive/CORBIS.